THERMO love

THE AUSTRALIAN
Women's Weekly

THERMO love

CONTENTS

KNOW YOUR THERMO *the essentials*

Thermo devices or "all-in-one"appliances have revolutionised the way many of us prepare and cook our daily meals. Much more than just a food processor, they can chop, grate, blend, puree, mill, grind, whip, sauté, boil, steam, weigh and more, often at the same time. A thermo is the busy cook's best friend, with its multi-layered cooking ability, hands-free stirring and set-and-forget functions. Plus, cleaning and mess is reduced to a minimum – what's not to like?

You will find your meal preparation will become faster and smarter – a delicious risotto can be gently stirring and simmering while you are busy with other things. No time to make a hot breakfast? Porridge can be cooking in your thermo while you make school lunches. Just got home from work and need to get dinner on the table fast? A healthy family-friendly meal can be cooked in under 30 minutes using a thermo.

For the health conscious and those who love to make meals from scratch, thermo devices have huge appeal. From grinding your own flours, making nut milks, butters and bread, to foolproof jams, custards and ice-creams, the list is endless.

There are a variety of brands and price ranges on the market and, as with any appliance, it is important to read your product's manual and safety instructions thoroughly before use.

We've separated the book into Weeknights (think delicious meals for the family in under 45 minutes) and Weekends (for recipes that take a little longer). From our Baking chapter you will be amazed at how easy it is to whip up a cake or bake some healthy bread rolls. And the steaming function will surprise you with its ability to produce a range of indulgent desserts. Snacks and drinks are a cinch to make in the thermo too, as are staples, such as bread, jam and passata.

DOS AND DON'TS

- **DO FAMILIARISE** yourself with your appliance and its functions before you start cooking.
- **DO REMEMBER** that cooking times are a guide. It's still important to check if food is cooked. Room temperature food will cook faster than food straight from the fridge.
- **DO ORDER** your cooking to minimise mess. Chop or mix dry foods before wet where possible.
- **DO PUT** harder foods in before soft when chopping.
- **DO PRESUME** the measuring cup in the lid is in place unless the recipe says to leave it off.
- **DO PAY ATTENTION** when steaming that there is sufficient water in the mixing bowl. Over long periods it may need topping up with boiling water.
- **DO TRY** and buy super fresh in-season fruit and vegetables for maximum flavour and nutrients.
- **DON'T OVERFILL** the mixing bowl; keep to the maximum fill level.
- **DON'T WORRY** about washing the mixing bowl between steps. We have tried to include this in the recipes if it is absolutely necessary.
- **DON'T BUY IT**, make it in the thermo instead. For example, to make icing sugar, mill white sugar for **20 sec/speed 10**, and to make rice flour, grind rice for **2 min/speed 10**.
- **DON'T BUY** a pre-made icing mix – make a simple buttercream in 3 minutes.
- **DON'T HAVE** mayonnaise? Whip up a batch in 2 minutes.

QUICK TEMPERATURE GUIDE

- **37°C** Gently warm food such as baby food and activate yeast.
- **40–55°C** Melt chocolate.
- **80–95°C** Slow cooking and gentle simmering, heat milk without boiling.
- **85–90°C** Cook custard, ice-cream bases, fruit curds and egg-based sauces.
- **100°C** Bring water to the boil, general cooking of soups, stews etc.
- **120°C** The highest temperature for most appliances. Use for toasting spices and sauteéing vegetable bases for soups, stews etc.
- **STEAM MODE** Use this mode when steaming in the steaming tray or steaming dish. With this function you will need at least 1 litre (4 cups) water in the mixing bowl. By adjusting the speed, the cooking time can be increased or decreased. Over long periods, the water in the mixing bowl may need to be topped up.

SPEEDY COOKING

- **STIR MODE** The slowest and gentlest of modes, similar to stirring with a wooden spoon. Use the reverse function to keep ingredients intact.
- **SPEEDS 1–3** For gentle mixing and combining soft ingredients such as mashed potato. Also for whipping cream or egg whites using the whisk attachment.
- **SPEEDS 4–6** For chopping hard vegetables, such as carrots, onions or beetroot. It's best if you first quarter onions and chop carrots into 5cm (2in) lengths. Also for crushing ice.
- **SPEEDS 7–10** For milling grains and grinding nuts and spices. For silky smooth pureeing of smoothies and soups. For chopping of chocolate, parmesan and other hard cheeses.
- **TURBO** Similar to the pulse button on a blender or food processor. For very powerful short bursts, this setting can be helpful to avoid over processing.
- **REVERSE MODE WITH SPEEDS 1–3** The blades turn in reverse, a gentle stir without chopping.
- **REVERSE MODE WITH SPEEDS 4–10** Useful for shredding vegetables such as cabbage without chopping.
- **DOUGH MODE** For kneading bread and pizza bases, or any dough where the gluten in the flour needs to be developed.

QUICK CHOP GUIDE

Remember, times will vary slightly depending on quantity. Machines will also vary, so start with 1–2 seconds less. You can go from rough chop to slush in a matter of seconds!

- **CHOP ONIONS** 5 sec/speed 5
- **CHOP SOFT HERBS** 5 sec/speed 7
- **GRATE CARROTS** 5 sec/speed 5
- **GRATE PARMESAN** 10 sec/speed 10
- **CHOP CHOCOLATE** 4 sec/speed 7
- **GRIND ALMONDS** 10 sec/speed 7
- **GRIND SPICES** 10–20 sec/speed 10
- **GRIND PEPPERCORNS** 60 sec/speed 10
- **GRIND SUGAR** 20 sec/speed 10

MIXING BOWL
STEAMING TRAY
STEAMING DISH
SIMMERING BASKET
SPATULA
WHISK ATTACHMENT

COOKING *made* SIMPLE

CRUSH

Mocktails, cocktails, slushies and smoothies – use your thermo for all these or to crush ice. Crush frozen chopped fruit for instant no-added-sugar fruity sorbets.

BEATING

Use the whisk attachment to aerate cream and egg whites, and to mix cake batters and egg-based sauces like custard. To beat egg whites, ensure the mixing bowl is clean.

MIX

The spatula can be used while the machine is in operation. Use it to scrape down the side of the bowl and push down on bulky ingredients to make contact with the appliance's blades.

CHOP

Chop fruits, vegies, chocolate and firm cheeses. For multiple types in the same recipe, place similar textures together. To mince meat, freeze 3cm (1¼in) pieces for 30 minutes first.

SAUTÉ

To sauté (just like in a frying pan), cook at **120°C/3–7 min/ stir mode**, depending on the volume and type of ingredients. Ingredients that are moister will cook faster.

SIMMERING BASKET

Use to steam vegies, grains and boil eggs, and as a sieve to drain food. Place over the hole in the mixing bowl lid to prevent splatters.

BLEND

Soups, smoothies, nut milks and much more – the thermo can be used as a powerful blender to achieve a silky creamy texture, or a coarser one, if you prefer.

Blend your own flours from nuts, grains or dried beans on speeds 9–10. You can also prepare spice mixes and grind your own coffee beans or any other hard dry ingredient.

STEAMING

Depending on the shape of the food that you are steaming, use either the steaming dish and/or tray, stacked, to steam fish, meat or vegetables. You can also steam eggs on the tray or in little cups. Set the appliance to steam mode.

KNEAD

Use the dough mode to take all the hard work out of making bread and pizza doughs.

COOK MODE

Set the timer, temperature and stir mode for general cooking. For soups, stews and risottos, cook at 120°C for initial sautéing and then at 100°C for the remaining time.

SNACKS & DRINKS

SWEET PEA & TARRAGON DIP
WITH SUPER SEED CRACKERS

prep + cook time *30 minutes* ***serves*** *8*
makes *2½ cups of spread & 45 crackers*

SUPER SEED CRACKERS

1⅔ cups (250g) plain (all-purpose) flour
25g (¾oz) pepitas (pumpkin seed kernels)
25g (¾oz) linseeds (flaxseeds)
25g (¾oz) sunflower seeds
15g (½oz) white sesame seeds
1 teaspoon sea salt flakes
1 teaspoon cracked black pepper
⅓ cup (80ml) extra virgin olive oil

SWEET PEA & TARRAGON DIP

100g (3oz) pecorino, cut into 2cm (¾in) cubes
500g (1lb) frozen peas, thawed
¼ cup (60ml) extra virgin olive oil, plus extra to serve
1 tablespoon loosely packed fresh tarragon leaves, plus extra to serve (see tips)

SUPER SEED CRACKERS

1 Preheat oven to 180°C/350°F. Line two large oven trays with baking paper.
2 Place all ingredients and ⅓ cup (80g) water in mixing bowl; mix for **15 sec/speed 3**. Knead for **2 min/dough mode**. Transfer to a lightly floured surface. Bring dough together to form a ball.
3 Halve dough. Roll one portion on a floured surface until 2–3mm thick; cut into small squares, approximately 4cm x 5cm (1½in x 2in) and place on prepared trays. Repeat with remaining dough.
4 Bake for 22 minutes or until light golden, swapping trays half way through cooking time. Cool crackers on trays.

SWEET PEA & TARRAGON DIP

1 Meanwhile, clean mixing bowl. Place pecorino in mixing bowl; grate for **8 sec/speed 9** or until finely grated. Add peas, oil and tarragon; mix for **1 sec/turbo** four times, scraping down the side of bowl when necessary, or until a coarse paste. Season to taste.
2 Drizzle dip with extra oil and sprinkle with extra tarragon. Serve dip with crackers.

tips Use ¼ cup mint leaves if tarragon is unavailable.
Crackers can be cooked in long sheets and broken into shards instead of cut into rectangles, if you prefer. Adjust the cooking time as necessary.

MAPLE CHILLI & TAHINI NUT CLUSTERS

***prep + cook time** 25 minutes* ***makes** 8 cups*

⅓ cup (80ml) tahini
⅓ cup (80ml) pure maple syrup
1½ teaspoons dried chilli flakes (see tip)
1½ teaspoons sea salt flakes
2 cups (320g) brazil nuts
1 cup (160g) blanched almonds
1 cup (120g) pecans
1 cup (150g) cashews

1 Preheat oven to 180°C/350°F. Line two large oven trays with baking paper.
2 Place tahini, maple syrup, chilli and salt in mixing bowl; cook for **3 min/100°C/stir mode** or until smooth and warm.
3 Add nuts to mixing bowl; mix for **3 sec/speed** 4 or until very coarsely chopped and some whole nuts are left.
4 Divide mixture between prepared trays. Bake for 20 minutes, turning and mixing the nuts every 10 minutes, or until golden and crisp. Cool completely on trays before storing in an airtight container.

tip For an extra spicy kick add another ½ teaspoon of chilli flakes.
keep Clusters will keep in an airtight container for up to 2 weeks.

CORN & MISO HUMMUS

prep + cook time 20 minutes serves 4 makes 2 cups

1 tablespoon black sesame seeds
¼ bunch coriander (cilantro), plus extra leaves to serve
1 trimmed corn cob (250g), kernels removed
2 green onions (scallions), trimmed, chopped
¼ cup (60ml) extra virgin olive oil
2 teaspoons ground cumin
400g (12½oz) can chickpeas (garbanzo beans), drained, rinsed
⅓ cup (80g) white (shiro) miso
1 clove garlic
2 limes (130g), finely zested, juiced
2 baby cos lettuce (romaine) (260g), leaves separated

1 Place sesame seeds in mixing bowl; heat for **4 min/120°C/reverse/stir mode.** Blend on **turbo/speed 1** four times until a coarse powder (see tip). Transfer to a small bowl and set aside. Rinse and dry mixing bowl.
2 Remove leaves from coriander and reserve. Cut stalks and roots into 4cm (1½in) pieces and add to mixing bowl; chop for **15 sec/speed 5** or until finely chopped. Add corn, green onion, 1 tablespoon of the oil and cumin to mixing bowl; cook for **7 min/120°C/reverse/stir mode** or until fragrant and softened slightly.
3 Add chickpeas, miso, garlic, remaining oil and 2 tablespoons of lime juice; blend for **40 sec/speed 6.5** or until smooth. Season to taste. Transfer to a small bowl and refrigerate until cool.
4 Sprinkle hummus with lime zest and sesame seed powder. Serve with baby cos lettuce leaves and reserved coriander leaves.

tip You may need to wait for the temperature to drop before using the turbo speed in step 1, as this function won't work at higher temperatures.
try with You could also serve the hummus with corn chips, crackers or flatbread, if you like.

NO-BAKE CHOC MUESLI BARS

prep time 25 minutes (+ refrigeration) ***makes 12***

25g (¾oz) golden linseeds (flaxseeds)
½ cup (70g) unsalted roasted macadamias
6 fresh dates (120g), pitted
1 cup (75g) shredded coconut
⅓ cup (55g) activated buckinis (buckwheat groats)
¼ cup (50g) pepitas (pumpkin seed kernels)
¼ cup (35g) sunflower seeds
¼ cup (40g) black chia seeds
80g (2½oz) cacao butter, chopped finely
¼ cup (70g) tahini
¼ cup (60ml) pure maple syrup
2 teaspoons vanilla extract
300g (9½oz) dark chocolate (70% cocoa), broken into pieces

1 Grease a 20cm (8in) square cake pan; line base and sides with baking paper, extending paper 5cm (2in) above sides.
2 Place linseeds in mixing bowl; mill for **30 sec/speed 9** or until finely ground. Scrape down the side of bowl. Add macadamias and dates; chop for **5 sec/speed 5** or until coarsely chopped. Transfer to a large bowl. Place coconut, buckinis, pepitas, sunflower and chia seeds in mixing bowl; mix for **10 sec/reverse/speed 2**. Add to the macadamia and date mixture.
3 Place cacao butter in mixing bowl; cook for **4 min/50°C/reverse/speed 2** or until melted, stopping after 2 minutes to scrape down the side of bowl. Add tahini, maple syrup and vanilla; heat for **2 min/50°C/reverse/speed 2** or until smooth. Pour over nut and seed mixture; mix until well combined.
4 Press mixture firmly and evenly over base of lined pan using a spatula. Refrigerate for 1 hour or until set.
5 Remove slice from pan; using a serrated knife, cut slice into 24 bars. Place bars on a baking-paper-lined tray and return to fridge.
6 Place chocolate in mixing bowl; chop for **8 sec/speed 7** or until finely chopped. Scrape down the side of bowl. Heat for **5 min/50°C/reverse/speed 2** or until chocolate is melted, stopping after 2 minutes to scrape down the side of bowl. Pour melted chocolate into a small wide glass; this will make it easier to dip the bars. Dip ends of bars, one at a time, into melted chocolate. Gently shake off excess chocolate. Return to tray and refrigerate for 10 minutes or until chocolate is set.

keep Bars can be refrigerated in an airtight container for up to 2 weeks.

CARROT & BEETROOT TZATZIKI
WITH WARM MARINATED OLIVES

prep + cook time 35 minutes serves 6

1½ tablespoons cumin seeds
4 cloves garlic
2 medium carrots (240g), cut into 5cm (2in) pieces
⅓ cup (80ml) extra virgin olive oil, plus extra to serve
1 medium beetroot (beet) (175g), trimmed, peeled, cut into eighths
2 teaspoons lemon juice
¼ cup fresh mint leaves, plus extra to serve
⅓ cup fresh dill, plus extra to serve
1¼ cups (350g) greek yoghurt
2 flatbreads (230g), warmed or char-grilled

WARM MARINATED OLIVES

1 clove garlic, sliced
2 large strips lemon rind
2 teaspoons fennel seeds
½ teaspoon dried chilli flakes
2 tablespoons fresh rosemary leaves
⅓ cup (80ml) extra virgin olive oil
2 fresh bay leaves
1 cup (160g) drained kalamata olives
1 cup (120g) drained green sicilian olives

1 Place cumin seeds in mixing bowl; mill for **40 sec/speed 8** or until finely ground. Add garlic; chop for **10 sec/speed 5** or until finely chopped. Remove half the garlic mixture to a small bowl and set aside. Add carrot to mixing bowl; chop for **8 sec/speed 5** or until coarsely chopped. Scrape down the side of bowl. Add half the oil; cook for **8 min/steam mode/reverse/speed 1** or until tender. Season. Transfer to a medium bowl to cool.
2 Place beetroot in mixing bowl; chop for **8 sec/speed 5** or until coarsely chopped. Scrape down the side of bowl. Add reserved garlic mixture and remaining oil to mixing bowl; cook for **10 min/steam mode/reverse/speed 1**. Season to taste. Stir in lemon juice. Transfer to a medium bowl to cool. Rinse and dry mixing bowl. Place herbs in mixing bowl; chop for **5 sec/speed 9**.
3 Stir yoghurt and chopped herbs evenly through the separate cooled carrot and beetroot mixtures. Chill until ready to serve.
4 Make warm marinated olives. Clean mixing bowl. Place garlic, lemon rind, fennel, chilli and rosemary in mixing bowl; chop for **10 sec/speed 8**. Scrape down the side of bowl. Add oil, bay leaves and both olives; cook for **5 min/90°C/reverse/stir mode** or until heated through.
5 Serve carrot and beetroot tzatziki drizzled with extra virgin olive oil and scattered with extra mint leaves and dill, with flatbreads and warm olives.

keep Olives can be stored for 2 weeks in an airtight container in the fridge. The oil will solidify when chilled; to rewarm, return to mixing bowl and heat for **4 min/90°C/reverse/stir mode**.

PAPAYA, MANGO & ALMOND SMOOTHIE

prep time 5 minutes *serves* 2

1 cup ice cubes
¼ cup (40g) natural almonds
½ small red papaya (300g), chopped
1 small mango (325g), cut into 5cm (2in) pieces (see tips)
1 cup (250ml) milk (see tips)
½ cup (140g) greek yoghurt (see tips)
1 teaspoon vanilla extract
1 tablespoon lime juice
2 teaspoons honey or pure maple syrup

1 Place ice in mixing bowl; blend for **30 sec/speed 9** or until crushed. Transfer to a container in the freezer.
2 Place almonds in mixing bowl; blend for **15 sec/speed 10** or until finely ground. Add remaining ingredients; blend for **1 min/speed 9** or until smooth. Serve over crushed ice, topped with a little honey and lime rind, if you like.

tips Use frozen mango or drained canned mango in natural juice, if fresh is not available.
For a dairy-free version, use a nut milk (see page 179) and soy or coconut yoghurt.
Blend ice with the ingredients for a thicker smoothie.

SUPER SEED BERRY SMOOTHIE

***prep time** 5 minutes (+ freezing)* ***serves** 2*

1 small banana (130g), cut into 5cm (2in) pieces
1 teaspoon linseeds (flaxseeds)
½ cup (140g) greek yoghurt
1 cup (150g) frozen mixed berries
1 tablespoon dried goji berries
1 tablespoon honey
1 cup (250ml) milk
1 teaspoon chia seeds

1 Place banana in an airtight container or resealable plastic bag. Freeze for 4 hours or until firm.

2 Place frozen banana and remaining ingredients in mixing bowl; blend for **1 min/speed 9** or until smooth.

3 Serve immediately, topped with extra linseeds, chia seeds and goji berries, if you like.

CHEESE & PORCINI MUSHROOM PUFFS

***prep + cook time** 50 minutes **makes** 18*

50g (1½oz) butter, chopped
¼ teaspoon sea salt flakes
½ cup (75g) plain (all-purpose) flour
2 eggs
olive oil cooking spray
¼ cup (20g) finely grated parmesan
15g (½oz) dried porcini mushrooms
350g (11oz) firm ricotta
75g (2½oz) soft goat's cheese
1 tablespoon fresh thyme leaves, plus extra sprigs to serve
2 teaspoons finely grated lemon rind

1 Place 100g (3oz) water, butter and salt in mixing bowl; heat for **3 min/100°C/speed 1** until butter is melted and mixture almost comes to the boil. Add flour; mix for **20 sec/speed 4**. Remove mixing bowl and set aside to cool for 5 minutes.
2 Preheat oven to 200°C/400°F. Line two large oven trays with baking paper.
3 Place mixing bowl back in position. Mix on **speed 5**, adding eggs one at a time through hole in mixing bowl lid. After adding the last egg, mix a further **30 sec/speed 5**.
4 Place mixture into a piping bag fitted with a 1.5cm (¾in) plain tube. Pipe 3cm (1¼in) rounds, about 5cm (2in) apart onto prepared trays. Use a dampened finger to smooth the tops. Bake for 10 minutes. Reduce oven to 180°C/350°F. Bake a further 10 minutes or until golden and puffed. Remove trays from oven.
5 With a small, sharp knife, make a small hole in the bottom of pastry. Return to trays, spray lightly with oil spray and scatter with parmesan. Bake for 5 minutes or until inside pastry is dry. Cool on trays.
6 Meanwhile, to make the filling, place mushrooms in a small bowl, cover with boiling water and stand for 5 minutes to soften; drain. Clean mixing bowl. Place mushrooms in mixing bowl; blend for **1 min/speed 9**. Scrape down the side of bowl. Add ricotta, goat's cheese, thyme and rind, then season to taste; blend for **10 sec/speed 7** or until smooth.
7 Place filling into a piping bag fitted with an 0.5cm (¾in) plain tube; pipe mixture into the cooled puffs. Sprinkle with extra thyme leaves to serve.

tip Puffs can be made a day ahead and stored in an airtight container. Puffs are best filled close to serving.
keep Unfilled puffs can be frozen for 2 months. Warm through gently in the oven to refresh puffs, then cool before filling.

GLUTEN-FREE ALMOND PIKELETS
WITH BLUEBERRY 'JAM'

***prep + cook time** 20 minutes (+ refrigeration)*
***makes** 10 pikelets & 1½ cups jam*

¾ cup (120g) natural almonds
¼ cup (45g) raw buckwheat groats
2 large ripe bananas (460g), halved
2 eggs
1 tablespoon pure maple syrup
1 teaspoon gluten-free baking powder
½ teaspoon ground cinnamon
1 cup (280g) greek yoghurt, to serve

BLUEBERRY 'JAM'

1 medium red apple (150g), cored, cut into 4cm (1½in) chunks
2 tablespoons pure maple syrup
1 tablespoon lemon juice
200g (6½oz) frozen blueberries
1 tablespoon white chia seeds

1 Make blueberry 'jam'. Place apple in mixing bowl; chop for **3 sec/speed** 7 until coarsely grated. Scrape down the side of bowl. Add maple syrup and lemon juice; cook for **4 min/100°C/speed** 2 until soft. Blend for **10 sec/speed** 6 or until a smooth puree. Add blueberries and chia seeds; cook for **3 min/100°C/reverse/speed** 2. Transfer to a jar and refrigerate for 30 minutes.
2 Meanwhile, place almonds and buckwheat in mixing bowl; grind for **10 sec/speed 9** or until finely ground. Add bananas, eggs, maple syrup, baking powder and cinnamon; mix for **15 sec/speed** 4 or until smooth.
3 Heat a large lightly greased non-stick frying pan over low heat. Working in batches of four, pour 2 tablespoons of batter into the pan. Cook for 1½ minutes or until bubbles appear and golden brown underneath. Turn and cook a further 1 minute or until golden and cooked through.
4 Serve pikelets topped with greek yoghurt and blueberry 'jam'.

try with You could also serve pikelets with ricotta, or if you are lactose intolerant, with coconut yoghurt.
keep Pikelets can be refrigerated for up to 2 days in an airtight container. Warm in the toaster or microwave before serving. 'Jam' will keep for up to 5 days.

'COCONUT ROUGH' POWER CUBES

prep time *5 minutes (+ refrigeration)* *makes* *20*

110g (3½oz) fresh dates, pitted
1 tablespoon dutch-processed cocoa
80g (2½oz) almond butter
150g (4½oz) dry-roasted almonds
65g (2oz) flaked coconut
50g (1½oz) dried cranberries
2 tablespoons rice malt syrup (see tip)

1 Line a 9cm x 25cm (3¾in x 10in) (top measurement) loaf pan with baking paper.
2 Place dates, cocoa and almond butter in mixing bowl; mix for **20 sec/speed 6**, scraping down the side of bowl halfway through mixing.
3 Add almonds and 50g (1½oz) of the coconut; mix for **7 sec/speed 6**. Add dried cranberries and rice malt syrup; mix for **1 sec/turbo**. Scrape down the side of bowl. Repeat until mixture comes together.
4 Press mixture into prepared pan. Press remaining coconut on top. Refrigerate until firm. Cut into squares to serve.

tip You could also use honey or maple syrup in place of rice malt syrup.
keep Power cubes can be frozen for up to 3 months.

SMOKED SALMON & CORIANDER SPREAD

prep + cook time 5 minutes *serves* 6

½ cup firmly packed fresh mint leaves
2 teaspoons cumin seeds
2 teaspoons coriander seeds
1 small red onion (100g), halved
250g (8oz) cream cheese, chopped
1 teaspoon finely grated lemon rind
200g (6½oz) smoked salmon
2 teaspoons extra virgin olive oil, plus extra to serve
crusty baguette or crackers, to serve

1 Reserve 1 tablespoon small mint leaves to serve. Place remaining mint in mixing bowl; blend for **6 sec/speed 8** or until very finely chopped. Transfer to a small bowl.

2 Clean and dry mixing bowl. Place cumin and coriander seeds in mixing bowl; cook for **2 min/120°C/speed 1**. Blend for **15 sec/speed** 7 or until coarsely ground.

3 Add red onion; chop for **6 sec/speed** 5 or until finely chopped.

4 Add cream cheese, lemon rind, salmon, oil and half the chopped mint; blend for **10 sec/speed 6** or until smooth. Scrape down the side of bowl. Blend a further **5 sec/speed 6**. Gently fold in remaining chopped mint to partially combine and create a ripple effect. Be careful not to overmix the mint into the spread.

5 Transfer spread to a serving bowl; scatter with reserved whole mint leaves and drizzle with extra oil. Serve with baguette slices.

FAST WEEKNIGHTS

SPAGHETTI RAMENAISE

prep + cook time 40 minutes (+ standing) serves 4

12 dried shiitake mushrooms (50g)
40g (1½oz) fresh ginger, sliced
4 cloves garlic
8 green onions (scallions), trimmed, quartered
2 tablespoons peanut oil
500g (1lb) minced (ground) pork
½ cup (120g) white (shiro) miso
1½ tablespoons dark soy sauce
1½ tablespoons sesame oil
200g (6½oz) frozen shelled edamame (soy beans), thawed
1½ tablespoons toasted sesame seeds
270g (8½oz) packet dried ramen noodles

1 Place mushrooms in a small bowl and pour over boiling water to cover; set aside for 30 minutes or until softened. Drain, reserving water. Slice mushrooms thinly, discarding stalks.
2 Meanwhile, place ginger and garlic in mixing bowl; chop for **10 sec/speed 9** or until finely chopped. Reserve 1 green onion; slice remaining green onions into 5cm (2in) lengths. Add sliced green onion to mixing bowl; chop for **5 sec/speed 5**. Scrape down the side of bowl. Add peanut oil; cook for **5 min/steam mode/reverse/stir mode** or until softened. Add pork and sliced mushroom; cook for **5 min/steam mode/reverse/stir mode,** stirring once halfway through cooking time to ensure there are no large lumps of mince, or until pork changes colour.
3 Add miso, soy sauce, sesame oil and ⅔ cup (160g) reserved mushroom water; cook for **10 min/steam mode/reverse/stir mode**. Add edamame and half the sesame seeds. Transfer to a bowl and cover to keep warm.
4 Rinse mixing bowl, then fill with 5 cups (1.25kg) water; cook for **10 min/steam mode/speed 1** or until boiling. Once boiling, remove measuring cup and add noodles, in batches, through the hole in lid, gently pushing down into water until submerged. Cook, with simmering basket in place of measuring cup, for **5 min/100°C/reverse/stir mode** or until al dente. Drain, then rinse under hot water to remove excess starch; drain well.
5 Combine noodles and mince mixture; divide among serving bowls. Sprinkle with remaining sesame seeds and reserved green onion, sliced thinly on the diagonal.

tip Veg it up by adding 60g (2oz) baby spinach leaves to noodles in the last minute of cooking time.

THAI-STYLE PORK LARB & NOODLES IN LETTUCE CUPS

prep + cook time 30 minutes serves 4

100g (3oz) dried rice vermicelli noodles
¼ bunch coriander (cilantro)
4 green onions (scallions), cut into 5cm (2in) lengths
40g (1½oz) fresh ginger, cut into quarters
2 cloves garlic
1 fresh long red chilli, halved, plus extra slices to serve
4 kaffir lime leaves, veins removed
2 teaspoons peanut oil
500g (1lb) minced (ground) pork
2 tablespoons fish sauce
3 tablespoons lime juice
1 small iceberg lettuce, leaves separated
¼ cup (60ml) sweet chilli sauce (optional)
lime wedges, to serve

1 Place vermicelli in a medium bowl and cover with boiling water; stand for 5 minutes, then drain well.
2 Reserve leaves from coriander for serving. Wash stems and roots; cut into 4cm (1½in) pieces. Place stems and roots, green onion, ginger, garlic, chilli, and lime leaves in mixing bowl; chop for **10 sec/speed 10**. Scrape down the side of bowl. Repeat process until paste is very fine. Add oil; cook for **5 min/steam mode/reverse/stir mode** or until fragrant.
3 Add pork; blend for **8 sec/reverse/speed 2** or until just combined. Cook for **5 min/100°C/reverse/stir mode** or until pork is cooked. Stir through fish sauce and lime juice.
4 Divide lettuce cups among plates, allowing two per serve. Top with noodles and pork mixture; drizzle with any juices. Sprinkle with reserved coriander leaves and extra chilli slices. Drizzle with sweet chilli sauce, if you like. Serve with lime wedges.

PRAWN LAKSA

prep + cook time 35 *minutes* *serves* 4

1 cup (300g) Laksa Paste (see page 103)
3 teaspoons vegetable oil
1kg (2lb) large uncooked prawns (shrimp), peeled, deveined, tails intact
2½ teaspoons fish sauce
1 teaspoon caster (superfine) sugar
400ml can coconut milk
450g (14½oz) fresh hokkien noodles
200g (6½oz) fried tofu puffs, halved
1 cup (80g) bean sprouts, trimmed
¼ cup loosely packed fresh coriander (cilantro) leaves
¼ cup loosely packed fresh mint leaves
1 tablespoon asian chilli oil (optional)

1 Make the laksa paste.
2 Add vegetable oil to paste in mixing bowl; cook for **10 min/100°C/speed 1** or until darkened slightly.
3 Fill mixing bowl with 5 cups (1.25kg) water; cook for **10 min/100°C/reverse/stir mode/speed 1** or until simmering.
4 Add prawns, fish sauce, sugar and coconut milk; cook for **5 min/100°C/reverse/stir mode/speed 1** or until prawns are just cooked.
5 Meanwhile, to heat noodles, place in a large bowl and cover with boiling water; set aside for 3 minutes. Gently separate with a fork, then drain.
6 Divide noodles and laksa among serving bowls; top with tofu puffs, bean sprouts, coriander and mint. Drizzle with chilli oil, if you like.

tip If short on time, you could use a purchased laksa paste instead of making it yourself.
keep You can easily double the laksa paste recipe. Store in the fridge for up to 2 weeks or freeze for 3 months. This will make mid-week laksas even faster to prepare.

CHANA MASALA
WITH CAULIFLOWER RICE

prep + cook time 40 *minutes* *serves* 4

1 large onion (200g), quartered
1 fresh long green chilli, deseeded, halved crossways
50g (1½oz) fresh ginger, chopped
2 cloves garlic
20g (¾oz) ghee (clarified butter)
1 teaspoon garam masala
1 teaspoon ground cumin
1 teaspoon ground turmeric
1 teaspoon ground coriander
½ teaspoon ground cardamom
2 x 400g (12½oz) cans diced tomatoes
¼ cup chopped fresh coriander (cilantro), plus extra to serve
2 x 400g (12½oz) cans chickpeas (garbanzo beans), drained, rinsed

TURMERIC CAULIFLOWER RICE

1 small cauliflower (1kg), cut into florets
1 teaspoon ground turmeric
20g (¾oz) ghee (clarified butter)

1 Prepare turmeric cauliflower rice. Working in four batches, place 250g (8oz) of the cauliflower into mixing bowl; chop for **8 sec/speed 5** or until finely chopped. Transfer to a bowl. Repeat with remaining cauliflower. Sprinkle chopped cauliflower with turmeric and mix to combine. Set aside. Rinse and dry bowl.
2 Place onion, chilli, ginger and garlic in mixing bowl; chop for **20 sec/ speed 4** or until finely chopped. Scrape down the side of bowl. Add ghee; cook for **5 min/steam mode/reverse/speed 1** or until softened. Scrape down the side of bowl. Add spices, season to taste and stir to combine; cook for **2 min/steam mode/reverse/speed 1** or until fragrant. Add tomatoes and coriander; stir to combine.
3 Place half the cauliflower in steaming dish, cover and position over mixing bowl; cook for **9 min/steam mode/reverse/speed 1** or until cauliflower is just tender. Transfer to a large bowl. Season to taste. Place remaining cauliflower in steaming dish; cook for **7 min/steam mode/ reverse/speed 1** or until just tender.
4 Add chickpeas to mixing bowl and stir to combine; cook curry for a further **5 min/100°C/reverse/stir mode**. Season to taste.
5 Meanwhile, wearing food-handling gloves, place cooled turmeric cauliflower in the centre of a clean tea towel; gather the ends together, twist and squeeze out as much moisture as possible. Transfer to a bowl and stir through ghee. Season to taste.
6 Serve curry with cauliflower rice, topped with extra coriander.

try this You could also serve the curry with broccoli rice. Follow the above method for the cauliflower rice, reducing the cooking time in step 3 to 4 minutes per batch.
keep Curry can be frozen for up to 3 months.

TRIPLE TREAT VEG MAC 'N' CHEESE

prep + cook time 45 minutes serves 4

125g (4oz) cheddar cheese, cut into 1cm (½in) pieces
80g (2½oz) parmesan, cut into 1cm (½in) pieces
400g (12½oz) butternut pumpkin, cut into 2cm (¾in) pieces
350g (11oz) cauliflower, cut into small florets
2 cloves garlic
3 cups (750ml) milk
250g (8oz) macaroni
1 bunch broccolini (175g), halved lengthways
¼ teaspoon ground nutmeg, plus extra to serve

1 Place cheeses in mixing bowl; blend for **10 sec/speed 7** or until the consistency of coarsely grated parmesan. Transfer to a small bowl.
2 Place pumpkin, cauliflower, garlic and milk in mixing bowl; cook for **25 min/100°C/speed 1**, without measuring cup inserted into lid, or until vegetables are soft. Return measuring cup to lid. Blend for **15 sec/speed 8** or until sauce is very smooth and silky.
3 Add pasta to mixing bowl through hole in lid; stir to combine. Position steaming dish over mixing bowl and cover. Cook for **14 min/steam mode/reverse/stir mode,** adding broccolini to steaming dish after 8 minutes, or until pasta and broccolini are al dente and sauce thickens.
4 Remove steaming dish. Add three-quarters of the grated cheeses and nutmeg to pasta mixture; stir to combine. Season to taste. Sprinkle mac 'n' cheese with remaining grated cheeses and extra nutmeg. Serve with broccolini.

MEXICAN MEATBALL, BEAN & CORN SOUP

prep + cook time 45 *minutes* *serves* 4

½ bunch coriander (cilantro)
500g (1lb) minced (ground) beef
2 x 35g (1oz) sachets taco seasoning mix
1 medium red onion (170g), quartered
1 medium red capsicum (bell pepper) (200g), cut into 8 pieces
1 tablespoon olive oil
500g (1lb) very ripe tomatoes, quartered
3 cups (750ml) chicken stock
2 trimmed corn cobs (500g)
2 x 400g (12½oz) cans four-bean mix, drained, rinsed
⅓ cup (80g) sour cream
tortilla chips, to serve

1 Remove the leaves from coriander and reserve for serving. Wash stems and roots; cut into 3cm (1¼in) pieces. Place stems and roots in mixing bowl; blend for **5 sec/speed 5** or until finely chopped. Transfer half the mixture to a small bowl and set aside. Add beef and 1 sachet seasoning mix to mixing bowl; blend for **5 sec/speed 10** or until combined. Transfer to a bowl. Roll tablespoons of mixture into 24 balls.

2 Place onion, capsicum and remaining chopped coriander in mixing bowl; chop for **5 sec/speed 5** or until coarsely chopped. Add oil and remaining taco seasoning; cook for **5 min/100°C/reverse/stir mode**. Add tomato; chop for **3 sec/speed 5**. Add stock. Place meatballs in simmering basket and insert in mixing bowl.

3 Place corn in steaming dish, cover and position over mixing bowl; cook for **20 min/steam mode/reverse/stir mode** or until corn and meatballs are tender.

4 Remove corn from steaming dish; cool slightly and cut kernels from cob in large shards. Divide meatballs among serving bowls. Stir beans through hot soup, then ladle over the meatballs; top with corn, a dollop of sour cream and reserved coriander leaves. Serve with tortilla chips.

MAYONNAISE

TRADITIONAL EGG MAYONNAISE

***prep time** 10 minutes **makes** 1¼ cups*

Place 2 egg yolks, 1 teaspoon dijon mustard, 1 tablespoon lemon juice, and salt and pepper to taste in mixing bowl; blend for **2 min/speed 4**, gradually adding combined ½ cup (125ml) olive oil and ½ cup (125ml) light olive oil through the hole in mixing bowl lid, drop by drop at first and then in a thin steady stream until mixture thickens. Season. Spoon into a jar and store in the fridge.

tip Make sure all the ingredients are at room temperature.

VARIATIONS

Blend the following ingredients into the finished traditional egg mayonnaise (see left) for **30 sec/speed 4**:

MISO MAYONNAISE Add 1 tablespoon white (shiro) miso and 1 teaspoon sesame oil.

LEMON MAYONNAISE Add 2 teaspoons finely grated lemon rind.

AÏOLI Add 2 cloves crushed garlic.

GREEN MAYONNAISE Add ½ cup of fresh mixed herb leaves such as mint, flat-leaf parsley or basil.

tip If the mayonnaise curdles, it is usually because the oil was added too fast. To rescue it, first try gradually adding 1 tablespoon boiling water; blend for **30 sec/speed 4** until the mayonnaise emulsifies again. If that doesn't work, transfer mayonnaise to a bowl. Place another egg yolk in mixing bowl; blend for **90 sec/speed 4** while very slowly adding mayonnaise until emulsified. If you prefer a thinner mayonnaise, add a little warm water.

try this As well as in sandwiches, use mayonnaise as a dipping sauce or to accompany grilled meats and fish. Use in potato salads with lots of fresh herbs.

GREEN GODDESS MAYO DRESSING

***prep time** 10 minutes **makes** ¾ cup*

Place ¼ cup egg mayonnaise, ¼ cup fresh flat-leaf parsley, 1 tablespoon each fresh basil leaves and fresh chopped chives, 1 tablespoon lemon juice, 2 tablespoons water, 1 anchovy fillet and 1 clove garlic in mixing bowl; blend for **30 sec/speed 5** or until smooth. Season. Add 2 tablespoons sour cream; blend for **10 sec/reverse/stir mode** until combined.

MEXICAN MAYO

***prep time** 5 minutes **makes** ¾ cup*

Place ¾ cup egg mayonnaise, 1 chilli in adobo sauce (or ½ teaspoon smoked paprika and ¼ teaspoon ground chilli) in mixing bowl; blend for **30 sec/speed 4** or until smooth. Transfer to a bowl and stir in ⅓ cup chopped fresh coriander (cilantro).

TOMATO MAYONNAISE

***prep time** 10 minutes **makes** 1¼ cups*

Place 1 cup egg mayonnaise, ¼ teaspoon smoked paprika and 1 teaspoon tomato paste in mixing bowl; blend for **30 sec/speed 4** or until smooth. Add 1 medium seeded quartered roma (egg) tomato; blend for **10 sec/reverse/stir mode** or until combined.

TARTARE SAUCE

***prep time** 10 minutes **makes** 1¼ cups*

Place 1 tablespoon drained capers and 4 small baby gherkins in mixing bowl; chop for **5 sec/speed 5** or until coarsely chopped. Add 1 cup egg mayonnaise, 1 tablespoon lemon juice, 2 teaspoons dijon mustard and 1 tablespoon chopped chives, then season; blend for **10 sec/reverse/stir mode** until combined.

BROAD BEAN & CAVOLO NERO RISOTTO

prep + cook time 30 minutes *serves* 4

100g (3oz) parmesan, cut into 1.5cm (¾in) cubes
1 medium white onion (150g), halved
1 clove garlic
1 tablespoon extra virgin olive oil
25g (¾oz) butter
1⅔ cups (335g) arborio rice
⅓ cup (80ml) white wine
2 teaspoons vegetable stock powder
6 large leaves cavolo nero (100g), stalks removed, leaves shredded (see tip)
500g (1lb) frozen broad (fava) beans, thawed, peeled
½ cup fresh mint leaves

1 Place parmesan in mixing bowl; grate for **8 sec/speed 9**. Transfer to a small bowl and set aside.
2 Place onion and garlic in mixing bowl; chop for **3 sec/speed** 7. Scrape down the side of bowl. Add oil and butter; cook for **2 min/ 100°C/speed 1** without measuring cup inserted into lid.
3 Insert butterfly whisk. Add rice and wine to mixing bowl; cook for **2 min/100°C/reverse/stir mode** without measuring cup inserted. Add 4 cups (1kg) water and stock powder; cook for **15 min/100°C/ reverse/stir mode** or until rice is al dente.
4 Place the cavolo nero in the bottom of a large serving bowl and pour in the risotto; cover and leave for 3 minutes. Add broad beans and half the parmesan, then season; stir gently and set aside for 2 minutes.
5 Scatter with remaining parmesan and mint to serve.

tip Cavolo nero is also sold as tuscan cabbage.

GINGER & GREEN ONION STEAMED FISH

***prep + cook time** 45 minutes (+ standing) **serves** 4*

10 green onions (scallions), trimmed
80g (2½oz) fresh ginger
800g (1½lb) thick white fish fillets
300g (9½oz) jasmine rice
150g (4½oz) snow peas, trimmed
150g (4½oz) sugar snap peas, trimmed
2 tablespoons sesame oil

SAUCE

60g (2oz) palm sugar, chopped
¼ cup (60ml) soy sauce
1 tablespoon chinese cooking wine (shao hsing)
1 tablespoon lime juice
2 teaspoons fish sauce
1 fresh long red chilli, sliced thinly

1 Cut 4 green onions into 6cm (2½in) lengths, then slice into julienne; place in iced water for 10 minutes or until curled. Remove from water and pat dry with paper towel. Meanwhile, thinly slice half the ginger and julienne the other half.
2 Line steaming tray with a piece of dampened baking paper. Lay remaining green onions (white part only) and sliced ginger on paper and place fish on top. Stack tray on top of steaming dish, cover and set aside.
3 Fill mixing bowl with 4 cups (1kg) cold water. Insert simmering basket and weigh rice. Remove simmering basket and rinse rice under cold running water. Return simmering basket to mixing bowl; cook for **15 min/ steam mode/speed 2**. Remove measuring cup from lid. Position steaming tray and dish over mixing bowl; cook for **12 min/steam mode/speed 2** or until fish is just cooked. Remove steaming tray and set aside. Place snow peas and sugar snap peas into steaming dish and cover; cook for **3 min/ steam mode/speed 2** or until vegetables are just tender and rice is cooked. Remove simmering basket and steaming dish from mixing bowl; keep warm.
4 Remove fish from steaming tray with a spatula, pat dry with paper towel and arrange on platter. Top with green onion curls and remaining julienned ginger. Heat sesame oil in a small saucepan over high heat for about 1 minute or until very hot (smoking). Carefully pour hot oil over steamed fish; it should make a sizzling sound as it cooks the spring onions and ginger.
5 Make the sauce. Discard water from mixing bowl and add palm sugar; chop for **10 sec/speed 5** or until finely chopped. Add remaining ingredients; cook for **1 min/steam mode/speed 2** or until sugar dissolves and sauce is hot. Spoon half the sauce over fish. Fluff rice with a fork and serve with fish, remaining sauce and vegetables.

BUTTER BEAN & KALE SOUP

prep + cook time 30 *minutes* *serves* 4

- **1 medium leek (350g), white part only, cut into 5cm (2in) pieces**
- **1 medium onion (150g), quartered**
- **1 medium carrot (120g), cut into 5cm (2in) pieces**
- **1 celery stalk (150g), cut into 5cm (2in) pieces**
- **2 cloves garlic**
- **2 teaspoons rosemary leaves**
- **1 tablespoon extra virgin olive oil**
- **½ teaspoon dried chilli flakes, plus extra to serve (optional)**
- **1 litre (4 cups) vegetable stock**
- **1 tablespoon lemon juice**
- **2 x 400g (12½oz) cans butter beans (lima beans), drained, rinsed**
- **200g (6½oz) kale, stalks removed, leaves chopped coarsely**
- **40g (1½oz) shaved parmesan, to serve**

1 Place leek, onion, carrot, celery, garlic and rosemary in mixing bowl; chop for **8 sec/speed 4** or until coarsely chopped. Scrape down the side of bowl. Add oil; cook for **5 min/steam mode/reverse/speed 1** or until softened.
2 Add chilli flakes and season; cook for **2 min/steam mode/reverse/speed 1** or until fragrant. Add vegetable stock and lemon juice; cook for **8 min/steam mode/reverse/stir mode**. Transfer half the soup to a large jug and set aside.
3 Add half the butter beans to soup in mixing bowl; blend for **30 sec/speed 9** or until smooth. Add unblended soup and remaining butter beans and combine using spatula; cook for **2 min/steam mode/reverse/stir mode** or until simmering. Add kale and combine using spatula; simmer for **3 min/steam mode/reverse/stir mode** or until kale is wilted. Season to taste.
4 Divide soup among serving bowls; sprinkle with parmesan and extra chilli flakes, if you like.

keep Soup can be frozen for up to 3 months. Add a little extra stock or water when reheating, if the soup has thickened.

HARISSA CHICKEN & COUSCOUS SOUP

prep + cook time 30 minutes serves 4

1 cup loosely packed fresh coriander (cilantro) leaves, plus extra to serve
1 cup loosely packed fresh mint leaves
1 cup loosely packed fresh flat-leaf parsley leaves
1 large red onion (300g), halved
1 clove garlic
1 teaspoon harissa paste
½ teaspoon ground turmeric
1 tablespoon olive oil
2 x 400g (12½oz) cans diced tomatoes
1 litre (4 cups) chicken stock
500g (1lb) chicken thigh fillets, cut into 4cm (1½in) pieces
½ cup (100g) couscous
1 teaspoon finely grated lemon rind
1 tablespoon lemon juice
lemon wedges and greek yoghurt, to serve

1 Place coriander, mint and parsley in mixing bowl; chop for **10 sec/speed 7** or until finely chopped. Scrape down the side of bowl. Transfer to a small bowl and set aside.

2 Place onion and garlic in mixing bowl; chop for **3 sec/speed 7**. Scrape down the side of bowl. Add harissa, turmeric and oil; cook for **4 min/120°C/speed 1**.

3 Add tomatoes, 3 cups (750ml) of the stock and the chicken; cook for **14 min/110°C/reverse/stir mode**.

4 Add couscous, lemon rind and juice, and chopped herbs; mix for **80 sec/reverse/speed 2**. Season to taste. Soup will thicken on standing, so thin soup with remaining stock.

5 Divide soup among serving bowls; scatter with extra coriander leaves. Serve with lemon wedges and greek yoghurt.

TOMATO, BASIL & BUFFALO MOZZARELLA OMELETTE

prep + cook time 25 *minutes* *serves* 4

⅓ cup firmly packed fresh flat-leaf parsley leaves
400g (12½oz) heirloom cherry tomatoes, halved
2 tablespoons extra virgin olive oil
1 small clove garlic, crushed
1 tablespoon lemon juice
8 eggs
4 egg whites
110g (3½oz) buffalo mozzarella, drained, torn
⅓ cup small fresh basil leaves
toast, to serve

1 Place parsley in mixing bowl; chop for **6 sec/speed 10** or until coarsely chopped. Remove half the parsley for the eggs. Place tomatoes in mixing bowl; chop for **3 sec/speed 5** or until roughly smashed. Transfer tomato mixture to a small bowl; add oil, garlic and lemon juice. Season to taste; stir to combine.
2 Rinse mixing bowl. Place eggs and whites in mixing bowl; blend for **8 sec/speed 8**. Transfer to a measuring jug. Stir through remaining parsley and season with salt and pepper.
3 Fill mixing bowl with 3 cups (750g) water; heat for **5 min/steam mode/speed 1**. Line steaming tray with a sheet of dampened baking paper; stack on top of steaming dish and position over mixing bowl. Carefully pour half the egg mixture onto the baking paper; cover and cook for **5 min/steam mode/speed 1** or until just set.
4 Remove steaming dish and tray. Transfer omelette to a large plate and cover to keep warm. Repeat with another sheet of dampened baking paper and remaining egg mixture.
5 Cut omelettes in half and divide among plates. Top with tomato mixture and torn mozzarella; fold omelettes over to cover. Scatter with basil leaves. Serve with toast.

SPICE BLENDS

JAMAICAN JERK SPICE MIX

prep + cook time *10 minutes* ***makes*** *½ cup*

Place 2 teaspoons whole allspice, ½ teaspoon black peppercorns, 2 cinnamon sticks, 2 small dried chillies and 1 teaspoon dried thyme in mixing bowl; cook for **5 min/120°C/speed 2** or until lightly toasted and fragrant. Blend for **30 sec/speed 10** or until finely ground. Transfer to a small bowl; stir in 2 teaspoons sweet paprika, 2 teaspoons dark brown sugar and 1 teaspoon salt flakes.

keep Store for 3 months in an airtight container in a cool spot out of direct sunlight.

FRAGRANT INDIAN-STYLE SPICE BLEND

prep + cook time *10 minutes* ***makes*** *½ cup*

Place 3 sticks cinnamon, 2 tablespoons cardamom pods, 1 tablespoon cloves and 1½ tablespoons garam masala in mixing bowl; cook for **2 min/120°C/speed 1**. Blend for **40 sec/speed 10** or until finely ground (discard any large cardamom husks). Transfer to a medium bowl; stir in 1½ tablespoons ground turmeric.

try this Rub over chicken, firm white fish or prawn skewers and cook on an oiled barbecue. You can also make three slashes on both sides of a whole fish, rub with the spice blend and some olive oil, then wrap in foil and either barbecue or bake.
keep Store for 3 months in an airtight container in a cool spot out of direct sunlight.

BERBERE-STYLE RUB

***prep + cook time** 10 minutes* ***makes** ½ cup*

Place 2 teaspoons coriander seeds, 1 teaspoon fenugreek seeds, seeds from 2 cardamom pods, 1 whole clove and 1 teaspoon whole black peppercorns in mixing bowl; cook for **5 min/ 120°C/speed 2** or until fragrant. Blend for **30 sec/speed 10** or until finely ground. Transfer to a jar; stir in ¼ cup sweet paprika, 2 tablespoons onion powder, ½ teaspoon each ground cinnamon and ground ginger, and ¼ teaspoon each ground allspice and nutmeg.

try this Rub into beef scotch fillet steaks and barbecue. It also goes well with chicken and lamb.
keep Store for 3 months in an airtight container in a cool spot out of direct sunlight.

PISTACHIO & CUMIN DUKKAH

***prep + cook time** 12 minutes* ***makes** ½ cup*

Place ⅓ cup (45g) shelled pistachios, 2 tablespoons white sesame seeds, 1 tablespoon coriander seeds, 1 tablespoon cumin seeds, 2 teaspoons fennel seeds and ½ teaspoon sea salt flakes in mixing bowl; cook for **10 min/ steam mode/speed 2**. Blend for **15 sec/speed 4** or until coarsely chopped.

try this Dukkah is traditionally served with bread and olive oil. First the bread is dipped in olive oil, then the dukkah. Dukkah is also delicious sprinkled over chicken, fish, lamb or eggs, before or after cooking.
keep Store for 3 months in an airtight container in a cool spot out of direct sunlight.

OLIVE PISTACHIO TROUT FILLETS
WITH PINK SLAW

prep + cook time 30 minutes serves 4

- 1 quantity of Sicilian Olive & Pistachio Tapenade (see page 87)
- 4 x 180g (5½oz) skinless, boneless ocean trout fillets (see tip)
- ½ small green cabbage (600g), cut into chunks
- 2 medium carrots (240g), cut into large chunks
- 2 medium beetroot (beets) (350g), peeled, quartered
- 3 green onions (scallions), sliced thinly
- ¼ cup fresh flat-leaf parsley leaves
- ½ cup (140g) greek yoghurt
- ⅓ cup (100g) mayonnaise
- 2 tablespoons lemon juice,
- 60g (2oz) rocket (arugula)
- lemon wedges, to serve

1 Make the tapenade.
2 Line steaming tray with baking paper. Arrange trout fillets, skin-side down, on paper. Spoon the tapenade evenly over tops of trout fillets, pressing to secure; season. Stack tray on top of steaming dish, cover and set aside.
3 Clean and dry mixing bowl. Place half the cabbage in mixing bowl; chop for **4 sec/speed 4** or until coarsely shredded. Transfer to a large bowl. Repeat with remaining cabbage. Place carrot and beetroot in mixing bowl; chop for **12 sec/speed 4** or until coarsely chopped. Add to bowl with cabbage along with green onion and parsley.
4 Add yoghurt, mayonnaise and lemon juice to vegetable mixture; mix well. Season to taste.
5 Fill mixing bowl with 4 cups (1kg) water; heat for **8 min/steam mode/speed 1** or until boiling. Position steaming dish and tray over mixing bowl; cook for **10 min/steam mode/speed 1** or until trout is just cooked through.
6 Serve trout with slaw, rocket and lemon wedges.

tip You could also use 2 chicken breasts, halved horizontally, in place of the trout. Cooking time will be the same.
keep Any leftover slaw will keep in an airtight container in the fridge for up to 3 days.

CHILLI PRAWN CHORIZO PENNE

prep + cook time *40 minutes* *serves* *4*

2 chorizo sausages (220g), peeled, cut into 3cm (1¼in) pieces
2 cloves garlic
1 medium onion (150g), halved
2 fresh long red chillies, chopped coarsely
400g (12½oz) can diced tomatoes
2 tablespoons tomato paste
⅓ cup (80ml) white wine
2 teaspoons caster (superfine) sugar
300g (9½oz) penne pasta
200g (6½oz) peeled uncooked prawns (shrimp), halved lengthways
fresh basil and shaved parmesan, to serve

1 Place chorizo in mixing bowl; chop for **5 sec/speed 6** or until finely chopped. Transfer to a small bowl and set aside.
2 Place garlic, onion and chillies in mixing bowl; chop for **3 sec/speed** 7. Cook for **3 min/steam mode/speed 1**.
3 Add tomatoes, tomato paste, wine, sugar and 2 cups (500g) water; cook for **10 min/100°C/speed 1**.
4 Add pasta and chopped chorizo; cook for **11 min/100°C/reverse/stir mode** or until pasta is almost al dente and sauce is thickened.
5 Add prawns; cook for **5 min/100°C/reverse/stir mode** or until prawns and pasta are just cooked. Season to taste.
6 Serve penne scattered with basil and parmesan.

tip Pasta sauce will thicken on standing; to loosen sauce, add a little boiling water.

RISONI
WITH CHICKEN & SALSA VERDE

prep + cook time 30 minutes *serves* 4

1 quantity Salsa Verde (see page 69)
600g (1¼lb) chicken breast fillets, cut lengthways into 4 strips
375g (12oz) risoni
lemon cheeks, to serve

1 Make the salsa verde.
2 Rinse mixing bowl, then fill with 4 cups (1kg) water; heat for **10 min/steam mode/speed 3** or until boiling. Place chicken on steaming tray and season; stack tray on top of steaming dish and cover. Add risoni to mixing bowl. Position steaming dish and tray over mixing bowl; cook for **10 min/steam mode/reverse/speed 2** or until chicken is cooked. Remove steaming dish and tray from mixing bowl. Check if risoni is cooked and, if necessary, cook a further **1–2 min/steam mode/reverse/speed 2**, without measuring cup inserted into lid, or until al dente.
3 Drain risoni and rinse under hot water to remove excess starch; transfer to a large bowl. Season to taste.
4 Serve risoni topped with sliced chicken and salsa verde, and with lemon cheeks.

try this Salsa verde is also a delicious accompaniment to grilled or roasted meat.
keep Any leftover salsa verde will keep for 2 weeks in the fridge.

ITALIAN-STYLE CREAMED CORN
WITH TOMATO & PROSCIUTTO

prep + cook time 35 minutes serves 4

260g (8½oz) ripe cherry truss tomatoes, removed from stalks
¼ cup (60ml) extra virgin olive oil
3 cloves garlic, bruised
1 tablespoon fresh thyme leaves, plus extra to serve
100g (3oz) parmesan, cut into large pieces
2 cups (320g) frozen corn kernels, thawed
1½ cups (225g) fine polenta
1 litre (4 cups) vegetable stock
100g (3oz) prosciutto slices
½ cup (125ml) pouring cream

1 Place tomatoes, oil, garlic and thyme in mixing bowl; cook for **10 min/100°C/speed 1**, without measuring cup inserted into lid, or until garlic and tomatoes are soft and almost broken down, or until a chunky sauce forms. Transfer to a small bowl and cover to keep warm.

2 Clean and dry mixing bowl. Place parmesan in mixing bowl; process for **10 sec/speed 8** or until finely grated. Transfer half to a small bowl and reserve for serving. Add corn, polenta and vegetable stock to mixing bowl; cook for **15 min/100°C/stir mode**, stirring after 7 minutes, or until polenta is tender and thickened. Season to taste.

3 Meanwhile, preheat grill (broiler) to high. Place prosciutto in a single layer on a foil-lined tray. Grill for 2 minutes each side or until crisp. Drain on paper towel and set aside to cool.

4 Add cream to mixing bowl; mix for **5 min/100°C/reverse/stir mode** or until heated through and almost smooth, with a few chunks of corn remaining for texture.

5 Divide creamed corn among serving bowls; top with tomato sauce, prosciutto and extra thyme. Serve with reserved parmesan.

HERB SAUCES

WALNUT BROCCOLI PESTO

prep + cook time 20 minutes ***makes*** *1 cup*

Fill mixing bowl with 4 cups (1kg) water; heat for **10 min/steam mode/speed 2** or until boiling. Place 200g (6½oz) broccoli florets in steaming dish, cover and position over mixing bowl; steam for **5 min/steam mode/speed 2** or until just tender. Transfer to a bowl of iced water, then drain and pat dry with paper towel. Rinse and dry mixing bowl. Place 2 strips lemon rind, 75g (2½oz) parmesan and 1 large clove garlic in mixing bowl; chop for **10 sec/speed 5** or until finely chopped. Add broccoli, ¼ cup (25g) toasted walnuts, ½ cup firmly packed fresh basil leaves, ½ cup firmly packed fresh flat-leaf parsley leaves and ¼ cup (60ml) extra virgin olive oil; chop for **5 sec/speed 5** or until coarsely chopped. Add another ¼ cup (60ml) oil and 2 teaspoons lemon juice; blend for **10 sec/speed 5** or until almost smooth. Season to taste. Transfer to a jar and store in the fridge.

try this Delicious tossed through pasta or dolloped on soups, sandwiches or barbecued meat, fish or vegetables.

NAM JIM

prep time 10 minutes ***makes*** *1 cup*

Place 3 cloves garlic, 3 seeded and quartered fresh long green chillies, ¼ cup fresh coriander (cilantro) leaves, 2 coriander (cilantro) roots, 2 tablespoons fish sauce, 2 tablespoons chopped palm sugar, 3 shallots cut into 5cm (2in) lengths and ¼ cup (60ml) lime juice in mixing bowl; blend for **20 sec/speed 10** or until smooth. Transfer to a jar and store in the fridge.

try this This Thai dipping sauce goes well with richer meats, such as barbecued pork or lamb. Use as a dipping sauce for prawns or toss through rice noodles for a Thai-style salad.

SALSA VERDE

prep time 10 minutes ***makes*** *1½ cups*

Using a vegetable peeler, remove rind from 1 small lemon, avoiding any white pith. Place lemon rind in mixing bowl; chop for **10 sec/ speed 8** or until finely chopped. Add 2 cups fresh basil leaves, 2 cups fresh flat-leaf parsley leaves, 1 bunch fresh chives cut into 4cm (1½in) lengths, 2 cloves garlic, 2 teaspoons dijon mustard, ½ cup (90g) drained cornichons and ½ cup (125ml) extra virgin olive oil to mixing bowl; chop for **4 sec/speed 6**. Scrape down the side of bowl; chop a further **5 sec/ speed 6**. Repeat if a finer salsa is desired. Transfer to a small bowl; stir in ¼ cup (45g) drained baby capers. Season to taste. Transfer to a jar and store in the fridge.

try this Use with our Risoni with Chicken & Salsa Verde on page 64. It also goes with barbecued or roast lamb, chicken, prawns and fish. Drizzle over char-grilled vegetables, or use instead of mayonnaise in sandwiches.

ZHUG

prep + cook time *10 minutes* ***makes*** *2 cups*

Place 2 teaspoons caraway seeds, 1 teaspoon cumin seeds, ½ teaspoon coriander seeds and the seeds from 6 cardamom pods in mixing bowl; cook for **5 min/120°C/speed 2** or until fragrant. Blend for **15 sec/speed 10** or until coarsely ground. Add 6 seeded and quartered fresh long green chillies, 4 cloves garlic, 1 cup firmly packed fresh coriander (cilantro) leaves, ½ cup firmly packed fresh flat-leaf parsley leaves, ⅓ cup (80ml) lemon juice and ½ cup (125ml) extra virgin olive oil; blend for **20 sec/speed 10** or until almost smooth. Transfer to a jar and store in the fridge.

try this This spicy, zesty and versatile sauce from Yemen goes with eggs, vegetables, seafood and meat.

ZUCCHINI & SPECK CARBONARA

prep + cook time 35 minutes serves 4

40g (1½oz) parmesan, cut into 2cm (¾in) pieces
40g (1½oz) pecorino, cut into 2cm (¾in) pieces, plus extra finely grated to serve
2 eggs
2 egg yolks
1.5 litres (6 cups) salt-reduced chicken stock
250g (8oz) speck, cut into 50g (1½oz) pieces
375g (12oz) linguine
2 medium zucchini (240g), halved crossways, cut into 3cm (1¼in) pieces

1 Place cheeses in mixing bowl; blend for **10 sec/speed 10** or until finely grated. Transfer to a medium bowl; add eggs and egg yolks, then stir until well combined. Set aside.

2 Place stock and speck in mixing bowl; cook for **11 min/100°C/reverse stir/speed 1** or until boiling. Remove the measuring cup and push pasta through the hole into the boiling stock; cook for **10 min/100°C/reverse stir/speed 1** or until pasta is al dente. Drain pasta and speck, reserving cooking liquid; set aside.

3 Place speck and zucchini in mixing bowl; blend for **3 sec/speed 6** or until finely chopped. Scrape down the side of bowl. Cook for **2 min/100°C/reverse/stir mode/speed 1** or until fragrant.

4 Add cooked pasta, ¼ cup (60g) reserved cooking liquid and cheese mixture; cook for **1 min/70°C/reverse/stir mode/speed 1** or until well combined and heated through (the eggs should be emulsified but not so hot that they scramble). Season to taste with plenty of pepper.

5 Serve carbonara immediately, sprinkled with extra finely grated pecorino.

tip Remaining pasta liquid can be used in soups or stews, if you like.

TOMATO SOUP
WITH CHEESY CROÛTONS

prep + cook time 25 *minutes* *serves* 4

100g (3oz) wedge of parmesan, including rind
5 cloves garlic
2 tablespoons fresh rosemary leaves, plus 1 teaspoon extra
⅓ cup (80ml) extra virgin olive oil
300g (9½oz) sourdough bread, crust removed, coarsely torn
1 medium red onion (170g), halved
3 x 400g (12½oz) cans diced tomatoes
1 cup (250ml) salt-reduced chicken stock
50g (1½oz) unsalted butter
1 teaspoon caster (superfine) sugar, or to taste

1 Preheat oven to 200°C/400°F. Line a baking tray with baking paper.
2 Remove rind from parmesan and reserve. Chop parmesan into 2cm (¾in) pieces. Place chopped parmesan in mixing bowl; blend for **10 sec/speed 10** or until finely grated. Transfer two-thirds to a small bowl and reserve.
3 To make croûtons, add 2 cloves garlic, rosemary and oil to remaining parmesan in mixing bowl; blend for **25 sec/speed 6** or until finely chopped and well combined. Add sourdough; mix for **25 sec/reverse/stir mode** or until well combined. Spread mixture evenly on prepared tray. Bake for 8 minutes, stirring halfway through cooking time, or until golden. Set aside.
4 Meanwhile, place onion, remaining garlic and extra rosemary in mixing bowl; blend for **6 sec/speed 5** or until finely chopped. Scrape down the side of bowl. Cook for **2 min/120°C/reverse/stir mode** or until softened. Add tomatoes, reserved parmesan rind and stock; cook for **10 min/100°C/reverse/speed 1** or until simmering. Remove parmesan rind. Add butter and sugar to taste; blend for **30 sec/speed 8** or until very smooth. Season.
5 Divide soup among serving bowls; scatter with croûtons and reserved grated parmesan.

tip Parmesan rinds can be frozen for up to 3 months. Gradually collect these (and pecorino rinds) and store in a large resealable plastic bag in your freezer.

FENNEL-RUBBED PORK
WITH SWEET POTATO PILAF

***prep + cook time** 45 minutes **serves** 4*

1 tablespoon fennel seeds
½ teaspoon sea salt flakes
500g (1lb) pork fillet, trimmed
500g (1lb) orange sweet potato, cut into 2cm (¾in) pieces
1 small onion (80g), quartered
1 medium fennel bulb (300g), trimmed, quartered, fronds reserved
2 cloves garlic
2 tablespoons moroccan seasoning
50g (1½oz) butter, chopped
3 cups (750ml) chicken stock
1½ cups (300g) brown basmati rice, rinsed
60g (2oz) baby spinach leaves

1 Place fennel seeds in mixing bowl; cook for **5 min/120°C/speed 2** or until fragrant. Add salt; blend for **5 sec/speed 10** or until coarsely chopped. Rub pork with fennel mixture and season with pepper. Place pork in steaming tray. Place sweet potato in steaming dish, in a single layer, in the centre of the dish. Stack steaming tray on top of dish, cover and set aside.

2 Place onion, fennel bulb, garlic and seasoning in mixing bowl; blend for **6 sec/speed 5** or until coarsely chopped. Add butter; cook for **5 min/steam mode/reverse/stir mode**. Add stock. Place rice in simmering basket and insert into mixing bowl.

3 Position steaming dish and tray over mixing bowl; cook for **22 min/steam mode/reverse/stir mode** or until pork, sweet potato and rice are just cooked. Stir rice in simmering basket with a fork halfway through cooking time.

4 Remove steaming dish and tray from mixing bowl. Remove simmering basket and drain rice well; transfer to a large bowl. Strain liquid mixture from the mixing bowl into a large bowl, reserving both liquid and solid fennel mixture.

5 Add fennel mixture, sweet potato and spinach to rice in bowl, then season; stir lightly to combine. Thickly slice pork and serve with pilaf, drizzled with a little reserved cooking liquid. Scatter with reserved fennel fronds.

keep Leftover cooking liquid can be frozen and used in soups, stews or sauces.

EASY WEEKENDS

COCONUT CHICKEN PILAF

***prep + cook time** 55 minutes* ***serves** 4*

2 medium red onions (340g), quartered
80g (2½oz) ghee (clarified butter)
2 cinnamon sticks
1 teaspoon ground turmeric
½ teaspoon ground cardamom
¼ cup (40g) raisins
2 chicken breast fillets (400g), cut into 3cm (1¼in) pieces
1 litre (4 cups) chicken stock
1½ cups (300g) white basmati rice
½ cup (80g) dry-roasted almonds, chopped coarsely
1 cup (50g) flaked coconut, toasted

1 Place onion in mixing bowl; chop for **8 sec/speed 4**. Scrape down the side of bowl. Add 40g (1½oz) of the ghee and the cinnamon sticks, then season; cook for 7 **min/100°C/reverse/speed 1** or until onion is softened.
2 Add turmeric, cardamom, raisins and 20g (¾oz) of the ghee; combine using spatula. Cook for **10 min/100°C/reverse/speed 1** or until golden brown and caramelised. Transfer to a bowl and set aside.
3 Add remaining ghee to mixing bowl; heat for **1 min/steam mode/reverse/stir mode** or until sizzling. Add chicken; cook for **3 min/steam mode/reverse/stir mode** or until almost cooked. Strain chicken juice into a jug and set aside chicken pieces.
4 Pour chicken juices and chicken stock into mixing bowl. Place rice in simmering basket and rinse under hot water; insert simmering basket into mixing bowl. Cook for **20 min/steam mode/speed 2** or until rice is tender.
5 Transfer cooked rice to a large bowl and fluff with a fork. Add caramelised onion mixture, chicken, half the almonds and half the coconut; season, then mix well to combine. Transfer to steaming dish.
6 Top up water in mixing bowl, if necessary, to make 1 litre (4 cups). Position covered steaming dish over mixing bowl; cook for **5 min/steam mode/speed 1** or until pilaf is heated through.
7 Transfer pilaf to a platter; scatter with remaining almonds and toasted coconut flakes.

CHIPOTLE MAPLE PULLED PORK BURGERS

prep + cook time 2 hours serves 6

2 teaspoons cumin seeds
2 medium ripe tomatoes (300g), quartered
½ cup (105g) chipotle in adobo sauce
¾ cup (180ml) orange juice
¼ cup (60ml) pure maple syrup
750g (1½lb) pork scotch fillet, cut into 5cm (2in) pieces
1 tablespoon olive oil
1 large onion (200g), sliced thinly
6 large bread rolls (450g), toasted
2 cups (50g) trimmed watercress sprigs

BUTTERMILK APPLE SLAW

⅓ cup (80ml) buttermilk
2 tablespoons egg mayonnaise (see tip)
1 tablespoon apple cider vinegar
2 teaspoons dijon mustard
2 green onions (scallions), cut into 4cm (1½in) lengths
¼ medium red cabbage (225g), chopped into 4cm (1½in) chunks
1 medium green apple (150g), quartered, cored
1 medium red apple (150g), quartered, cored

1 Place cumin in mixing bowl; cook for **2 min/steam mode/speed 2** or until fragrant and lightly toasted. Mill for **10 sec/speed 9**. Add tomatoes, chipotle in adobo sauce, orange juice and maple syrup; blend for **10 sec/speed 6** or until smooth.

2 Season pork. Heat oil in a large frying pan over high heat; cook pork, in batches, for 2 minutes each side until browned. Transfer to a plate. Add ⅓ cup (80ml) water to frying pan; cook for 2 minutes, stirring and scraping with a wooden spoon, until reduced by half. Add to mixing bowl along with pork and onion; cook for **80 min/100°C/reverse/stir mode** or until pork is very tender and can be pulled apart with a fork.

3 Use tongs to remove pork to a large bowl. Use two forks to gently shred meat. Cook sauce for **15 min/steam mode/speed 3**, with simmering basket in place of measuring cup, until reduced by half. Return pork to mixing bowl; cook for **1 min/steam mode/reverse/stir mode** to heat through. Transfer to a bowl and cover to keep warm.

4 Make buttermilk apple slaw. Clean mixing bowl. Place buttermilk, mayonnaise, vinegar and mustard in mixing bowl; blend for **20 sec/speed 6**. Season to taste. Add green onion; chop for **3 sec/speed 4**. Add cabbage and apples; chop for **3 sec/speed 4**. Scrape down the side of bowl. Chop for **2 sec/speed 4** or until coarsely chopped.

5 Top bread roll bases with watercress and slaw, spoon over pork mixture, then top with bread roll tops.

tip You can make our Traditional Egg Mayonnaise on page 46 for this recipe, if you like.

STICKY CHINESE
PORK RIBS

***prep + cook time** 1 hour 30 minutes* ***serves** 4*

2kg (4lb) American-style pork ribs, cut into individual ribs
1½ cups (300g) jasmine rice
250g (8oz) choy sum, trimmed, cut into 7cm (2¾in) lengths

SAUCE

2 cloves garlic
50g (1½oz) fresh ginger, chopped
1 cup (360g) honey
½ cup (125ml) soy sauce
¼ cup (60ml) chinese cooking wine (shao hsing)
¼ cup (60ml) rice wine vinegar
2 green onions (scallions), sliced thinly
4 star anise
2 cinnamon sticks

1 Make the sauce. Place garlic and ginger in mixing bowl; chop for **5 sec/speed 5** or until finely chopped. Add honey, soy sauce, cooking wine, vinegar, green onion, star anise and cinnamon sticks; combine using spatula. Cook for **3 min/steam mode/reverse/speed 1** or until almost boiling. Cook a further **5 min/90°C/reverse/speed 1**, without measuring cup inserted into lid, or until fragrant. Pour into a small bowl and refrigerate for 30 minutes or until sauce cools and thickens slightly.
2 Meanwhile, divide ribs among lightly oiled steaming tray and steaming dish. Stack tray on top of dish, cover and set aside.
3 Fill mixing bowl with 4 cups (1kg) cold water; insert simmering basket and weigh rice. Remove simmering basket and rinse rice under cold running water. Return simmering basket to mixing bowl. Position steaming dish and tray over mixing bowl; steam for **30 min/steam mode/speed 2** or until rice is cooked. Transfer cooked rice to a serving bowl and cover to keep warm. Stir ribs to rotate; cook a further **30 min/steam mode/speed 2** or until tender. Transfer ribs to a large bowl.
4 Preheat grill (broiler) to high. Reserve ½ cup (125ml) sauce for serving. Pour remaining sauce over ribs and stir to coat. Arrange ribs on two foil-lined oven trays; grill for 12 minutes, turning every 2 minutes, or until sticky and dark.
5 Meanwhile, top up mixing bowl with hot water to make 2 cups (500ml), if necessary. Place choy sum in steaming dish. Position covered steaming dish over mixing bowl; cook for **5 min/steam mode/speed 1** or until choy sum is just tender.
6 Arrange ribs on a platter; spoon over reserved sauce. Serve with steamed rice, choy sum and fresh sliced red chilli in soy sauce, if you like.

PRAWN & LEMONGRASS CURRY

prep + cook time 45 minutes *serves* 4

2 tablespoons tomato paste
400ml can coconut cream
1 tablespoon fish sauce
2 tablespoons lime juice
20g (¾oz) palm sugar, chopped
500g (1lb) jap pumpkin, cut into 1.5cm (¾in) pieces
1kg (2lb) large uncooked prawns (shrimp), peeled, deveined, tails intact
150g (4½oz) snow peas, trimmed
450g (14½oz) microwave white rice
1 lime (65g), cut into wedges

CURRY PASTE

2 stalks lemongrass (40g), white part only, chopped
2 kaffir lime leaves, leaves torn, plus extra finely shredded to serve
2 cloves garlic
40g (1½oz) fresh ginger, chopped
1 fresh long red chilli, deseeded, halved crossways
1 medium onion (150g), quartered
1 tablespoon extra virgin olive oil

1 Make curry paste. Place lemongrass and lime leaves in mixing bowl; chop for **10 sec/speed 8** or until finely chopped. Scrape down the side of bowl. Add garlic, ginger and chilli; chop for **30 sec/speed 5** or until finely chopped. Add onion; chop for **10 sec/speed 5** or until finely chopped. Scrape down the side of bowl. Add oil; cook for 7 **min/steam mode/reverse/speed 1** or until softened.

2 Add tomato paste, coconut cream, fish sauce, lime juice and palm sugar; blend for **30 sec/speed 9** or until smooth. Scrape down the side of bowl.

3 Place pumpkin in steaming tray; stack tray on top of steaming dish, cover and position over mixing bowl. Cook for **18 min/steam mode/reverse/speed 2** or until pumpkin is almost tender. Place prawns in simmering basket and insert into mixing bowl. Return steaming dish and tray with pumpkin to mixing bowl; cook for **3 min/steam mode/reverse/speed 1**. Scatter snow peas over pumpkin; cover and steam for **3 min/steam mode/reverse/speed 1** or until vegetables are tender and prawns are cooked through.

4 Add prawns, pumpkin and snow peas to curry sauce in mixing bowl; gently combine using spatula.

5 Microwave rice according to packet directions.

6 Top curry with extra finely shredded lime leaves. Serve with steamed rice and lime wedges.

keep Curry can be frozen for up to 2 months.

TAPENADES

PROVENÇAL TAPENADE

prep time 15 minutes makes 1¾ cups

Place 2 cloves garlic and 1 strip lemon rind in mixing bowl; chop for **10 sec/speed 10** or until finely chopped. Add 2 cups pitted kalamata olives, 3 drained anchovy fillets, 1 tablespoon rinsed and drained capers, ½ cup firmly packed fresh flat-leaf parsley leaves and ¼ cup firmly packed fresh oregano leaves; chop for **5 sec/ speed 5** or until finely chopped. Scrape down the side of bowl. Add ½ cup (125ml) olive oil; blend for **4 sec/speed 5** or until almost smooth. Transfer to an airtight container and store in the fridge.

try this Spread over char-grilled bread and top with tomato, or use as an omelette filling with goat's cheese, or in a sandwich with hard-boiled eggs and cress.

GREEN OLIVE, CHILLI & MACADAMIA TAPENADE

prep time 15 minutes makes 2 cups

Place ½ cup firmly packed fresh flat-leaf parsley leaves and 1 small clove garlic in mixing bowl; chop for **10 sec/speed 10** or until finely chopped. Add 3 drained anchovy fillets, 2 trimmed dried long red chillies, ½ cup roasted macadamias, 2 teaspoons lemon juice and ¼ cup (60ml) extra virgin olive oil; blend for **5 sec/speed 5** or until finely chopped. Scrape down the side of bowl. Add 1⅓ cups (180g) pitted green olives; blend for **5 sec/ speed 4** or until almost smooth. Season to taste. Transfer to an airtight container and store in the fridge.

tip The heat level from the chillies is quite mild; to reduce it further, seed the chillies first. You could substitute dried chillies with 1 fresh long red chilli, if you like.

try this Use as a dip with crackers, toss through a roasted sweet potato salad with grilled fish or lamb, or dollop on steamed potatoes.

SICILIAN OLIVE & PISTACHIO TAPENADE

***prep time** 15 minutes* ***makes** 1 cup*

Place 1 cup (180g) pitted sicilian olives, 1 cup fresh flat-leaf parsley leaves, ⅓ cup (80ml) extra virgin olive oil and 45g (1½oz) Pistachio & Cumin Dukkah (see page 59 for recipe and tip below) in mixing bowl; mix for **5 sec/speed 5** or until a medium fine paste.

tip If you are short of time, use a purchased dukkah.
try this Toss through pasta with roasted cherry tomatoes, use in sandwiches with chicken or char-grilled vegetables, or as an accompaniment for grilled or steamed fish.

FIG TAPENADE

***prep time** 10 minutes* ***makes** 1 cup*

Place 1 clove garlic, 3 anchovy fillets and 1½ tablespoons drained capers in mixing bowl; blend for **5 sec/speed 5** or until finely chopped. Add 12 trimmed and quartered dried figs and 2 cups fresh flat-leaf parsley leaves; blend for **10 sec/speed 5** or until finely chopped. Add 2 teaspoons red wine vinegar and ⅓ cup (80ml) extra virgin olive oil; blend for **5 sec/speed 2**. Season with pepper.

try this Use as an accompaniment for roasted or barbecued steak, lamb, pork or duck.

BEEF RENDANG
WITH CHILLI SAMBAL

prep + cook time 3 hours serves 4

1 cup (75g) shredded coconut, plus extra toasted to serve
1 tablespoon vegetable oil
750g (1½lb) beef brisket, cut into 5cm (2in) pieces
2 large onions (400g), cut into 4cm (1½in) chunks
8 dried chillies (40g)
30g (1oz) fresh ginger, chopped coarsely
5 cloves garlic
2 stalks lemongrass (40g), white part chopped, long green stems knotted
6 kaffir lime leaves
1 tablespoon coconut sugar
500g (1lb) baby new (chat) potatoes, halved
1 tablespoon fish sauce
1 medium lime (90g), rind finely grated (reserve for sambal), juiced
roti or steamed rice, to serve

CHILLI SAMBAL

5 fresh long red chillies, chopped coarsely
10g (½oz) fresh ginger, chopped coarsely
3 cloves garlic
⅓ cup (80ml) white vinegar
½ cup (110g) caster (superfine) sugar
2 teaspoons finely grated lime rind

1 Make chilli sambal. Place chillies, ginger and garlic in mixing bowl; chop for **5 sec/speed 7**. Scrape down the side of bowl. Add vinegar; cook for **5 min/120°C/speed 1**. Blend for **10 sec/speed 4**. Add sugar; cook for **5 min/120°C/speed 1** until mixture thickens and slightly caramelises. Stir in lime rind; season with salt. Transfer to a bowl.

2 To make coconut milk, clean mixing bowl. Place shredded coconut in mixing bowl and cover with 2½ cups (625g) boiling water; cook for **8 min/steam mode/speed 1**. Blend for **30 sec/speed 10** or until smooth. Pour into a jug and set aside.

3 Meanwhile, heat oil in a large frying pan over high heat; cook beef, in batches, for 5 minutes, turning on all sides until evenly browned. Season. Transfer to a plate.

4 Clean mixing bowl. Place onion, chilli, ginger, garlic and chopped lemongrass in mixing bowl; chop for **5 sec/speed 7**. Scrape down the side of bowl. Add the pan juices from searing the beef; cook for **10 min/steam mode/speed 1** or until vegetables are soft.

5 Add the coconut milk, beef, 4 lime leaves, coconut sugar and knotted lemongrass stems to mixing bowl; season. Place potatoes in steaming dish, cover and position over mixing bowl; cook for **120 min/100°C/reverse/stir mode**.

6 Check if beef and potatoes are cooked; cook a further **15 min/100°C/reverse/stir mode** until both are very tender, adding roti to potatoes in steaming dish to warm through in last 2 minutes of cooking time. Beef is cooked when it can be shredded with a fork. Stir in fish sauce and lime juice to taste.

7 Transfer potatoes to a serving bowl; top with beef rendang. Scatter with finely shredded remaining lime leaves and extra coconut. Serve with roti or steamed rice, chilli sambal and extra lime wedges, if you like.

LAMB KOFTAS
WITH TABBOULEH & GARLIC TOUM

prep + cook time 35 minutes serves 4

500g (1lb) diced lamb shoulder, chilled (see tip)
½ medium red onion (85g), halved
½ cup (70g) slivered almonds
½ bunch fresh mint leaves, plus extra to serve
2 cloves garlic
2 teaspoons ground cumin
1 teaspoon mixed spice
2 teaspoons honey
1 tablespoon extra virgin olive oil
4 lebanese flatbreads (460g)

CHOPPED TABBOULEH

½ cup (80g) fine burghul
½ medium red onion (85g), cut into 4cm (1½in) pieces
½ bunch fresh mint leaves
1 telegraph (hothouse) cucumber (400g), cut into 4cm (1½in) pieces
250g (8oz) cherry tomatoes
2 tablespoons lemon juice

GARLIC TOUM

8 large cloves garlic
2 tablespoons lemon juice
1 teaspoon sea salt flakes
1 egg white
¾ cup (180ml) light olive oil

1 Place half the lamb in mixing bowl; chop for **0.5 sec/turbo** eight times or until the consistency of chunky mince. Transfer to a medium bowl. Repeat with remaining lamb.
2 Place onion, almonds, mint, garlic and spices in mixing bowl; chop for **5 sec/speed 5** or until a grated consistency.
3 Preheat grill (broiler) to high. Return mince to mixing bowl. Add honey and season well; mix for **20 sec/speed 3** or until well combined. Shape heaped tablespoons of mixture into balls and place on a foil-lined oven tray. Drizzle with oil. Grill for 10 minutes, turning halfway through cooking time, until evenly browned and cooked through. Transfer to a plate and cover to keep warm.
4 Meanwhile, make chopped tabbouleh. Wash and dry mixing bowl thoroughly. Place burghul in a heatproof bowl and cover with 1 cup (250ml) boiling water; set aside for 10 minutes until water is absorbed. Drain well on paper towel to absorb excess water. Place onion and mint in mixing bowl; chop for **3 sec/speed 7**. Add cucumber and tomatoes; chop for **2 sec/speed 5** until coarsely chopped. Strain. Transfer to a bowl; add burghul and lemon juice. Season to taste. Combine well with spatula.
5 Make garlic toum. Wash and dry mixing bowl. Place garlic, 1 tablespoon of the lemon juice and salt in mixing bowl; chop for **8 sec/speed 7**. Scrape down the side of bowl. Repeat until smooth. Add egg white; blend for **10 sec/speed 5**. Mix for **2 min/speed 4**, gradually pouring oil and remaining lemon juice through hole in lid, until well emulsified.
6 Serve koftas, tabbouleh and extra mint in flatbreads, drizzled with garlic toum.

tip To save time, use good-quality lamb mince instead of making your own, and buy a ready-made garlic dip instead of making the toum.

SLOW-COOKED BEEF POT PIES
WITH ROOT VEG MASH

***prep + cook time** 1 hour 25 minutes* ***serves** 4*

1 medium onion (150g), halved
2 cloves garlic
2 tablespoons extra virgin olive oil
1 large carrot (180g), cut into 1cm (½in) pieces
1 celery stalk (150g), cut into 1.5cm (¾in) pieces
3 teaspoons fresh thyme leaves
2 tablespoons tomato paste
¼ cup (60ml) red wine vinegar
1 tablespoon dijon mustard
1 tablespoon golden syrup
3 teaspoons beef stock powder
400g (12½oz) diced tomatoes
750g (1½lb) gravy beef, cut into 3cm (1¼in) pieces
½ cup (60g) frozen peas
1 quantity Root Vegetable Mash (see page 176) (see tip)
40g (1½oz) butter, chopped

1 Place onion and garlic in mixing bowl; chop for **5 sec/speed 5**.
2 Add oil, carrot, celery and thyme; cook for **3 min/100°C/reverse/stir mode**.
3 Add tomato paste, vinegar, mustard and golden syrup; cook for **2 min/100°C/reverse/stir mode** without measuring cup inserted into lid.
4 Add stock powder, tomatoes and beef; cook for **60 min/100°C/reverse/stir mode**, with simmering basket in place of measuring cup, or until beef is tender. Transfer to a large bowl. Stir in peas. Cover to keep warm.
5 Make the root vegetable mash.
6 Preheat grill (broiler) to high. Divide meat mixture among four 1⅔-cup (410ml) ovenproof dishes; top with mash and dot with butter. Grill for 5 minutes or until mixture is hot and topping is golden.

tip You could use potato mash instead of root vegetable mash, if you like.

KOREAN
SHORT RIB BAO

prep + cook time 2 hours 30 minutes (+ standing) serves 4

1kg (2lb) beef short ribs, cut into 4cm x 3cm (1½in x 1¼in) rib pieces (see tips)
1 medium onion (150g), quartered
1 medium nashi pear (200g), quartered
5 cloves garlic
½ cup (125ml) soy sauce
⅓ cup (120g) honey
2 tablespoons gochujang (korean chilli paste) (see tips)
1 teaspoon sesame oil
¼ cup (60ml) rice wine vinegar
350g (11oz) daikon, cut into 2cm (¾in) pieces
1 medium carrot (120g), julienned
½ bunch green onions (scallions) (200g), sliced thinly lengthways
8 large bao buns, to serve
1 tablespoon sesame seeds, toasted
coriander (cilantro) leaves, to serve

1 Soak beef ribs in cold water for 1 hour; drain well.
2 Meanwhile, place onion, pear and garlic in mixing bowl; blend for **10 sec/speed 6** until a chunky puree. Scrape down the side of bowl. Add ½ cup (125g) water, soy sauce, honey, gochujang, sesame oil and 2 tablespoons of the vinegar; cook for **5 min/steam mode/speed 2** or until simmering.
3 Drain ribs and add to mixing bowl with daikon; cook for **120 min/100°C/reverse/stir mode** or until meat falls off the bone and can be shredded with a fork.
4 Strain mixture, reserving both solids and liquid; discard bones. Shred meat with two forks. Return liquid to mixing bowl; cook for **15 min/steam mode/speed 3**, without measuring cup inserted into lid, or until reduced by half. Add enough of the sauce to shredded meat mixture to bind.
5 Combine remaining vinegar, the carrot and green onion in a small bowl; season.
6 Serve beef mixture with warm bao buns (see tips) and carrot mixture, scattered with sesame seeds and coriander leaves, drizzled with the remaining sauce.

tips Ask your butcher to cut the ribs crossways through the bone into shorter pieces, to make it easier to fit them into the mixing bowl.
Gochujang is a spicy, savoury and sweet fermented chilli paste that adds a real depth of flavour to this dish. It is available in Asian grocery stores and some supermarkets.
You can heat the bao buns in the steaming dish while the sauce is reducing.

PRAWN & HALOUMI PIZZA

***prep + cook time** 40 minutes (+ standing)* ***makes** 2*

1 quantity Basic Bread Dough (see page 172)
1 cup (250ml) bottled tomato passata (see tips)
¼ cup (60ml) olive oil
750g (1½lb) uncooked medium king prawns (shrimp), peeled, deveined
375g (12oz) haloumi, grated
400g (12½oz) mixed cherry tomatoes, quartered
½ cup fresh oregano leaves
1 small clove garlic, crushed
2 cups rocket (arugula)

1 Make step one of the bread dough.
2 Preheat oven to 220°C/440°F.
3 Knock down dough. Divide into two portions. On a lightly floured surface, roll one portion out to a 35cm (14in) round. Place on a 35cm (14in) pizza tray. Spread half the passata over dough, leaving a 1cm (½in) border. Repeat with remaining dough and passata. Bake for 10 minutes, swapping trays between shelves halfway through cooking time.
4 Combine 1 tablespoon of the oil and the prawns in a medium bowl; season. Top pizzas with the prawn mixture and haloumi. Bake for 15 minutes, swapping trays between shelves, if necessary, or until bases are browned and crisp underneath and prawns are cooked.
5 Meanwhile, to make salsa, combine tomatoes, oregano, garlic and remaining oil in a small bowl; season with salt and pepper.
6 Serve pizzas topped with tomato salsa and rocket.

tips You can also make the passata on page 183 for this recipe, if you like. Add a pinch of chilli flakes to salsa for an extra flavour kick.

GADO GADO SALAD

***prep + cook time** 40 minutes **serves** 4*

- ½ cup (75g) unsalted roasted cashews, plus extra to serve (see tip)
- 1 small clove garlic
- 1 tablespoon rice wine vinegar
- 1 tablespoon kecap manis
- 1 tablespoon soy sauce
- 400ml can coconut milk
- 4 eggs, chilled
- 400g (12½oz) baby new (chat) potatoes, quartered
- 150g (4½oz) green beans
- ¼ small red cabbage (200g), cut into chunks
- ¼ small wombok (napa cabbage) (175g), cut into chunks
- 4 small red radishes (60g), quartered
- coriander (cilantro) leaves, to serve

1 To make satay sauce, place cashews and garlic in mixing bowl; chop for **10 sec/speed 5** or until finely chopped. Add vinegar, kecap manis, soy sauce and coconut milk; cook for **10 min/steam mode/reverse/speed 2** or until combined and thickened slightly. Transfer to a medium bowl and set aside.

2 Clean mixing bowl. Place 2 cups (500g) water in mixing bowl. Place eggs and potatoes in simmering basket and insert into mixing bowl. Place beans in steaming dish and position over mixing bowl. Cover and cook for **15 min/steam mode/speed 1**. After 7 minutes, if beans are tender, remove steaming dish with beans and insert measuring cup into lid; continue cooking eggs and potatoes. Run beans under cold running water to refresh. Remove simmering basket and run eggs and potatoes under cold running water to stop further cooking. Peel eggs and halve.

3 Dry mixing bowl. Place red cabbage in mixing bowl; chop for **5 sec/speed 3** or until chopped coarsely. Transfer to a large bowl. Repeat with wombok.

4 Arrange cabbages, egg, potato, beans and radishes on a large platter; scatter with extra cashews and coriander leaves. Serve with satay sauce.

tip You could also replace the cashews with roasted peanuts for a more traditional version.

SLOW-COOKED LAMB
WITH PECORINO & CREAMY SEMOLINA

***prep + cook time** 2 hours 30 minutes **serves** 4*

60g (2oz) pecorino, cut in half
2 cups fresh flat-leaf parsley leaves
1 clove garlic
1 medium lemon (140g), rind finely grated, juiced
1 teaspoon cumin seeds
1 teaspoon ground coriander
2 tablespoons honey dijon mustard
1.1kg (2¼lb) boneless lamb shoulder
mixed salad leaves, to serve

CREAMY SEMOLINA

1¼ cups (200g) coarse semolina
30g (1oz) butter
2 small cloves garlic, sliced thinly
2 teaspoons vegetable stock powder

1 Place pecorino in mixing bowl; chop for **10 sec/speed 10** or until finely grated. Transfer to a small bowl. Place parsley and garlic in mixing bowl; chop for **10 sec/speed 10** or until finely chopped. Transfer to bowl with grated pecorino, add lemon rind and combine.

2 In a large bowl, combine cumin, coriander, mustard and lemon juice, then season; mix well. Add lamb; use hands to rub spice mixture all over lamb.

3 Fill mixing bowl with 6 cups (1.5kg) hot water. Line steaming tray with a piece of baking paper 5cm (2in) larger than the tray. Place lamb and marinade, in a single layer, on paper. Stack tray on top of steaming dish, cover and position over mixing bowl. Cook for **120 min/steam mode/speed 2**, topping up boiling water after 1 hour, or until very tender.

4 Preheat oven to 250°C/480°F. Line a shallow baking dish with foil. Carefully remove lamb from steaming tray and place on prepared tray; reserve juices. Cook lamb in oven for 10 minutes or until skin is crispy and caramelised.

5 Meanwhile, make creamy semolina. Clean and dry mixing bowl. Place semolina in a small jug. Place butter and garlic in mixing bowl, then season; cook for **30 sec/100°C/speed 1**. Add stock powder and 800g (1½lb) water; cook for **5 min/80°C/speed 2**, while slowly pouring semolina through the hole into the mixing bowl.

6 Carefully strain lamb juices into a small saucepan. Bring to the boil; simmer for 10 minutes or until thickened slightly. Season to taste.

7 Serve lamb sliced or shredded with creamy semolina, drizzled with lamb juices and sprinkled with pecorino mixture. Serve with salad leaves.

CURRY PASTES

RED CURRY PASTE

***prep + cook time** 25 minutes (+ standing)*
***makes** 1 cup*

Place 20 dried long red chillies in a small heatproof bowl, cover with boiling water and stand for 15 minutes; drain. Meanwhile, place 1 teaspoon ground coriander, 2 teaspoons ground cumin and 1 teaspoon hot paprika in mixing bowl; cook for **5 min/steam mode/reverse/stir mode** or until fragrant. Add drained chillies, 2cm (¾in) ginger, 3 cloves garlic, 1 medium quartered red onion, 1 sliced stalk lemongrass (white part only), 2 tablespoons chopped coriander (cilantro) roots and stems, 2 teaspoons shrimp paste and 1 tablespoon peanut oil; blend for **40 sec/speed 8** or until a smooth paste, scraping down the side of bowl halfway through blending. Transfer to an airtight container and refrigerate for up to 2 weeks.

try this Use this paste in red curries using barbecued duck, pineapple and tomato or as the base for stir-fries and soups, especially with pumpkin.

GREEN CURRY PASTE

***prep + cook time** 25 minutes*
***makes** 1 cup*

Place 2 teaspoons each coriander seeds and cumin seeds in mixing bowl; heat for **5 min/steam mode/speed 1** or until fragrant. Blend for **10 sec/speed 8** or until finely ground. Add 10 coarsely chopped fresh long green chillies, 1 teaspoon shrimp paste, 1 clove garlic, 4 green onions (scallions) cut into 4cm (1½in) lengths, 1 coarsely chopped stalk lemongrass (white part only), 1cm (½in) piece fresh galangal, ¼ cup coarsely chopped fresh coriander root and stems, and 1 tablespoon peanut oil; blend for **40 sec/speed 8**, scraping down the side of bowl halfway through blending, or until smooth. Transfer to an airtight container and refrigerate for up to 2 weeks.

try this Use this paste with green curries using chicken or fish.

YELLOW CURRY PASTE

prep + cook time *25 minutes (+ standing)*
makes *1 cup*

Place 2 dried red chillies in a small heatproof bowl, cover with boiling water and stand for 15 minutes; drain. Meanwhile, place 1 teaspoon each ground coriander and ground cumin, and ½ teaspoon ground cinnamon in mixing bowl; heat for **5 min/steam mode/reverse/speed 1** or until fragrant. Add drained chillies, 2 quartered fresh yellow banana chillies, 1 teaspoon chopped fresh turmeric, 2 cloves garlic, 1 quartered small onion, 1 chopped stalk lemongrass (white part only), 1 tablespoon sliced fresh galangal, 1 tablespoon coarsely chopped fresh coriander root and stem, 1 teaspoon shrimp paste and 1 tablespoon peanut oil; blend for **40 sec/ speed 8**, scraping down the side of bowl halfway through blending, or until smooth. Transfer to an airtight container and refrigerate for up to 2 weeks.

tip You can substitute the ground coriander and ground cumin seeds for whole seeds in this recipe; blend for **10 sec/speed 8** or until finely ground, before adding the chillies.
try this Use this paste with milder curries using chicken, beef or seafood, and in combination with coconut milk or cream.

LAKSA PASTE

prep time *20 minutes (+ standing)*
makes *1 cup*

Place 7 long red dried chillies in a small heatproof bowl, cover with boiling water and stand for 20 minutes; drain. Remove seeds. Place drained chillies, 2 trimmed and deseeded fresh long red chillies, 2 teaspoons shrimp paste, 1 medium quartered red onion, 5 cloves garlic, 3cm (1¼in) piece fresh ginger, 2 chopped stalks fresh lemongrass (white part only), 1 teaspoon ground turmeric, 2 tablespoons ground coriander and 1 tablespoon water in mixing bowl; blend for **40 sec/speed 7** or until a smooth paste forms. Transfer to an airtight container and refrigerate for up to 2 weeks.

try this Use this paste in our Prawn Laksa recipe on page 38.

INDIAN SLOW-COOKED CHICKEN CURRY

***prep + cook time** 1 hour 20 minutes* ***serves** 4*

4 small chicken marylands (1kg) (see tips)
2 tablespoons tandoori paste
40g (1½oz) fresh ginger, chopped coarsely
4 cloves garlic
1 medium onion (150g), quartered
2 tablespoons Fragrant Indian-style Spice Blend (see page 58)
50g (1½oz) unsalted butter
2 fresh long green chillies, pricked with a sharp knife (optional)
2 tablespoons tomato paste
400ml can coconut milk
400g (12½oz) can cherry tomatoes
⅓ cup fresh coriander (cilantro) leaves
⅓ cup fresh mint leaves
⅓ cup (15g) flaked coconut
steamed rice (see tips) and lime wedges, to serve

1 Rub chicken all over with half the tandoori paste until well covered; season. Set aside.

2 Place ginger and garlic in mixing bowl; blend for **5 sec/speed 8** or until finely chopped. Add onion; blend for **6 sec/speed 5** or until finely chopped. Scrape down the side of bowl. Add spice blend, butter and green chillies; cook for **5 min/120°C/reverse/stir mode** until softened. Add tomato paste and remaining tandoori paste; cook for **2 min/120°C/reverse/stir mode** until darkened slightly.

3 Reserve 2 tablespoons of the coconut milk; cover and chill until required. Add remaining coconut milk, the tomatoes, marinated chicken and ½ cup (125g) water to mixing bowl; cook for **60 min/100°C/reverse/stir mode** until chicken is very tender, removing measuring cup from lid halfway through cooking time. Season to taste. Transfer curry to a large bowl and cover to keep warm.

4 Drizzle curry with reserved coconut milk; scatter with coriander, mint and coconut flakes. Serve with steamed rice and lime wedges.

tips If your chicken maryland pieces are too large to fit in the mixing bowl, cut through the leg joint to form two pieces.
To save time, use a 450g (14½oz) packet of microwave rice.

JERK SALMON
WITH PINEAPPLE SALSA

prep + cook time 1 hour 5 minutes *serves 6*

1 bunch fresh coriander (cilantro)
3 medium limes (270g)
50g (1½oz) fresh ginger, sliced thickly
½ medium red onion (85g), quartered
1 fresh long red chilli, sliced
½ medium ripe pineapple (625g), cut into 6cm (2½in) pieces
1kg (2lb) centre-cut piece boneless salmon, skin on
2 tablespoons Jamaican Jerk Spice Mix (see page 58 and tip)
½ cup (125ml) extra virgin olive oil
6 corn cobbettes (425g), halved
1¼ cups (250g) pearl barley, soaked in boiling water for 30 minutes
400g (12½oz) baby green beans, trimmed, halved lengthways
2 teaspoons caster (superfine) sugar
400g (12½oz) can black beans, drained, rinsed
200g (6½oz) grape tomatoes, halved

1 To make the pineapple salsa, pick leaves from coriander stalks and reserve for serving. Coarsely chop ¼ cup stalks. Using a vegetable peeler, remove rind from 2 limes, avoiding the white pith. Juice all the limes and reserve. Place lime rind in mixing bowl; blend for **20 sec/speed 8** or until finely chopped. Scrape down the side of bowl. Transfer half the rind to a small bowl and reserve. Add ginger to mixing bowl; blend for **20 sec/speed 8** or until finely chopped. Add chopped coriander stalks; chop for **10 sec/speed 5** or until finely chopped. Add red onion and chilli; chop for **3 sec/speed 5** or until coarsely chopped. Add pineapple; chop for **2 sec/speed 3** or until coarsely chopped. Transfer to a medium bowl; stir in 1 tablespoon of the reserved lime juice. Season to taste; set aside.
2 Place a piece of dampened baking paper in steaming tray. Place salmon on paper, trimming slightly to fit, if necessary. Rub jerk spice mix all over salmon, drizzle with 2 tablespoons of the oil and season. Place corn in steaming dish. Stack tray on top of dish, cover and set aside.
3 Fill mixing bowl with 5 cups (1.25kg) water. Place drained barley in simmering basket and insert into mixing bowl; cook for **15 min/steam mode/speed 4**.
4 Position steaming dish and tray over mixing bowl; cook for **20 min/steam mode/speed 2** or until barley is tender and salmon is just cooked to your liking (cooking time will depend on thickness of salmon). Add green beans to the corn in the last 3 minutes of cooking time.
5 Meanwhile, combine ⅓ cup remaining reserved lime juice, the sugar, reserved lime rind and remaining oil in a small jug; season to taste. Combine black beans, tomatoes and half the lime dressing in a large bowl.
6 Add barley, corn and beans to black bean mixture, then season well; transfer to a large platter. Carefully transfer salmon and any juices to platter; drizzle with remaining dressing. Top with reserved coriander leaves, if you like. Serve with pineapple salsa.

tip If you don't have time to make the jerk spice mix, buy a ready-made cajun spice blend.

MUSHROOM & FETTA ARANCINI BALLS

***prep + cook time** 1 hour 20 minutes* ***makes** 24*

80g (2½oz) parmesan, halved
1 small onion (80g), halved
75g (2½oz) butter
1½ cups (300g) arborio rice
1 litre (4 cups) chicken stock
200g (6½oz) swiss brown mushrooms
2 shallots (50g)
100g (3oz) marinated fetta, drained
2 teaspoons fresh thyme leaves, chopped
¼ cup (20g) sage and onion stuffing mix
⅓ cup (50g) plain (all-purpose) flour
3 eggs, beaten lightly
1½ cups (115g) panko (japanese) breadcrumbs
light olive oil, for deep-frying
1 medium lemon (140g), cut into wedges

1 Place parmesan in mixing bowl; grate for **10 sec/speed 10**. Transfer to a small bowl; set aside. Place onion in mixing bowl; chop for **5 sec/speed 5**. Scrape down the side of bowl. Add 50g (1½oz) of the butter to mixing bowl; cook for **3 min/120°C/reverse/stir mode** without measuring cup inserted into lid.
2 Insert butterfly whisk in mixing bowl. Add rice and stock; scrape bottom of mixing bowl well with spatula to loosen rice. Cook for **20 min/100°C/reverse/stir mode** without measuring cup inserted into lid. Add parmesan to mixing bowl and stir to combine.
3 Spread mixture out on a large tray lined with baking paper; refrigerate for 20 minutes until cool.
4 Meanwhile, clean mixing bowl. Place mushrooms and shallots in mixing bowl; chop for **10 sec/speed 4**. Add remaining butter; cook for **5 min/120°C/reverse/stir mode** or until soft. Transfer to a medium bowl to cool, then add fetta, thyme and stuffing mix; stir to combine.
5 Roll 2 tablespoons rice mixture into balls; with moistened fingers, flatten balls slightly. Top balls with 2 teaspoons of mushroom mixture; enclose rice around mixture to seal. Repeat with remaining rice and filling.
6 Coat balls in flour, shaking off excess. Dip in egg, then coat in breadcrumbs. Fill a medium saucepan two-thirds full with oil; heat over medium heat to 180°C/350°F or until a cube of bread turns golden in 2 minutes. Cook balls, in three or four batches, for 2 minutes, turning occasionally, or until golden. Drain balls on paper towel. Serve with lemon wedges.

tip You can prepare balls up to the end of step 5 a day ahead. Refrigerate in an airtight container until ready to use. Increase the cooking time to allow balls to completely heat through when frying.

SWEDISH MEATBALLS
WITH GRAVY & HORSERADISH MASH

prep + cook time 1 hour 20 minutes serves 4

1 medium onion (150g), quartered
¾ cup fresh dill sprigs
200g (6½oz) minced (ground) beef
200g (6½oz) minced (ground) pork
½ cup (50g) fresh breadcrumbs
1 egg
2 teaspoons ground allspice
½ whole nutmeg, grated finely
1 quantity Mashed Potato
(see page 176)
¼ cup (65g) bottled horseradish
2 tablespoons olive oil
lemon wedges, to serve

GRAVY

1½ cups (375ml) beef stock
30g (1oz) unsalted butter
2½ tablespoons plain (all-purpose) flour
⅓ cup (80ml) pouring cream
2 teaspoons worcestershire sauce

1 To make the meatballs, place onion and ½ cup of the dill sprigs in mixing bowl; chop for **5 sec/speed 8** or until finely chopped. Scrape down the side of bowl. Add beef, pork, breadcrumbs, egg, allspice and nutmeg, then season well; mix for **20 sec/reverse/speed 4** or until well combined. Roll tablespoons of mixture into balls and place on a tray; cover and refrigerate until needed.

2 Make the mashed potato; add horseradish and stir to combine. Transfer to a bowl and cover to keep warm.

3 Heat oil in a large frying pan over medium-high heat; cook meatballs, turning, for 5 minutes until browned all over. Transfer to steaming tray and dish. Stack tray on top of dish, cover and set aside.

4 Clean mixing bowl, then fill with 4 cups (1kg) water; heat for **10 min/steam mode/speed 2**. Once boiling, position steaming dish and tray over mixing bowl; cook for **20 min/steam mode/speed 2** or until meatballs are cooked through. Remove steaming dish and tray; keep warm while you make the gravy.

5 Make the gravy. Clean mixing bowl. Place all ingredients in mixing bowl; cook for **8 min/90°C/speed 4** or until hot and thickened. Season to taste.

6 Serve meatballs on mash, drizzled with gravy and scattered with remaining dill, with lemon wedges to the side.

RICOTTA & OREGANO GNOCCHI
WITH PEPPERONI & OLIVE SAUCE

prep + cook time 35 minutes serves 4

- 120g (4oz) parmesan, rind removed, cut into 3cm (1¼in) pieces
- 500g (1lb) firm ricotta, well drained (see tip)
- 1 egg
- 1 egg yolk
- ¼ cup fresh oregano leaves
- ⅔ cup (100g) plain (all-purpose) flour
- 1 medium onion (150g), quartered
- 30g (1oz) pepperoni, sliced
- 2 tablespoons extra virgin olive oil
- 2 x 400g (12½oz) cans diced tomatoes
- 200g (6½oz) grape tomatoes, halved
- ⅓ cup (55g) pitted kalamata olives
- 150g (4½oz) baby spinach leaves

1 Place parmesan in mixing bowl; grate for **8 sec/speed 9** or until finely grated. Transfer 40g (1½oz) to a small bowl and reserve. Add ricotta, egg, yolk and 2 tablespoons of the oregano, then season well with salt and pepper; mix for **5 sec/speed 5**. Scrape down the side of bowl. Repeat until well combined. Add flour; mix for **5 sec/speed 4** or until just combined. Do not overmix.

2 Transfer mixture to a large bowl. Using floured hands, shape tablespoons of mixture into balls. Transfer balls to lightly oiled steaming tray and steaming dish. Stack tray on top of dish, cover and refrigerate until needed.

3 Clean mixing bowl. Place onion and pepperoni in mixing bowl; chop for **5 sec/speed 5** or until coarsely chopped. Add oil; cook for **8 min/steam mode/reverse/stir mode** without measuring cup inserted into lid. Add canned tomatoes, grape tomatoes, olives and remaining oregano; season. Position steaming dish and tray over mixing bowl; cook for **15 min/steam mode/reverse/stir mode** or until gnocchi are tender. Remove steaming dish and tray; keep warm.

4 Add spinach to mixing bowl and season; cook for **2 min/steam mode/reverse/stir mode** or until spinach is wilted.

5 Serve gnocchi with sauce and spinach, sprinkled with reserved parmesan.

tip Use ricotta from the deli and not the tubs from the supermarket.

PULLED BEEF BOLOGNESE
WITH PAPPARDELLE

***prep + cook time** 2 hours 30 minutes **serves** 4*

100g (3oz) wholemeal sourdough bread, torn coarsely
2 tablespoons fresh rosemary
⅓ cup (80ml) extra virgin olive oil
3 cloves garlic
840g (1¾lb) beef cheeks, sinew removed, cut into 3cm (1¼in) pieces
½ cup (125ml) red wine
1 medium onion (150g), halved
1 medium carrot (120g), trimmed, quartered
1 celery stalk (150g), trimmed, quartered
2 x 400g (12½oz) cans diced tomatoes (see tip)
1 cup (250ml) beef stock
375g (12oz) pappardelle
2 tablespoons coarsely chopped fresh flat-leaf parsley leaves
shaved parmesan, to serve (optional)

1 Place bread, half the rosemary, 1 tablespoon of the oil and 1 clove garlic in mixing bowl; blend for **5 sec/speed 8** or until finely chopped. Heat a large heavy-based frying pan over medium heat; cook breadcrumb mixture for 4 minutes, stirring often, or until golden and crisp. Transfer to a tray lined with paper towel to cool.
2 Heat another 1 tablespoon of the oil in same pan over medium-high heat; cook beef, in two batches, for 3 minutes, turning occasionally, or until browned and caramelised all over. Return beef to pan and season. Add wine and scrape the base of pan; cook for 30 seconds. Set aside.
3 Meanwhile, place vegetables and remaining rosemary, oil and garlic in mixing bowl; mix for **10 sec/speed 6** or until very finely chopped.
4 Add meat and any juices, tomatoes and stock to mixing bowl, then season; cook for **120 min/110°C/reverse/stir mode**, without measuring cup inserted into lid, or until meat is very tender. Transfer bolognese to a large bowl. Using two forks, pull beef apart. Cover to keep warm.
5 Rinse mixing bowl and fill with 8 cups (2kg) salted water; heat for **8 min/steam mode/reverse/stir mode** or until boiling. Add pasta, pressing down with lid, if necessary; cook for **8 min/100°C/reverse/stir mode**, stirring pasta after 4 minutes. Drain well.
6 Add pasta to bolognese sauce and toss gently to combine. Serve topped with breadcrumb mixture, parsley and parmesan.

tip Instead of 2 x 400g cans diced tomatoes, you can use 800ml tomato passata. See recipe on page 183 to make your own.

BOSTON-STYLE BEANS

***prep + cook time** 40 minutes* ***serves** 4*

1 medium onion (150g), quartered
150g (4½oz) speck, rind removed, cut in 2cm (¾in) pieces
2 cloves garlic
1 tablespoon extra virgin olive oil
1 tablespoon golden syrup
1 tablespoon dijon mustard
400g (12½oz) can diced tomatoes
1 cup (250ml) vegetable stock
1 fresh bay leaf
3 x 400g (12½oz) cans borlotti beans, drained, rinsed (see tip)
¼ cup fresh flat-leaf parsley leaves
toasted bread or Oat & Seed Rolls (see page 152), to serve

1 Place onion, speck and garlic in mixing bowl; chop for **4 sec/speed 5**. Add oil; cook for **5 min/100°C/speed 1** without measuring cup inserted into lid.
2 Add remaining ingredients, except for the beans and parsley; cook for **30 min/100°C/stir mode**, without measuring cup inserted into lid, or until thickened.
3 Add beans; cook a further **3 min/100°C/reverse/speed 0.5**, without measuring cup inserted.
4 Serve beans scattered with parsley, with toasted bread or rolls.

tip You can substitute any canned beans for the borlotti beans.
try this These beans make a great breakfast with poached or boiled eggs.

DESSERTS

HAZELNUT & CHOCOLATE ICE-CREAM TERRINE

***prep + cook time** 20 minutes (+ cooling & freezing)* ***serves** 8*

2½ cups (625ml) milk
¾ cup (180ml) thickened (heavy) cream
9 free-range egg yolks
⅔ cup (145g) caster (superfine) sugar
¼ cup (60ml) hazelnut-flavoured liqueur
skinless roasted hazelnuts, chopped coarsely, to serve
dutch-processed cocoa, to serve

CHOCOLATE HAZELNUT SPREAD

1 cup (135g) skinless roasted hazelnuts
¼ cup (25g) dutch-processed cocoa
1 teaspoon vanilla bean paste
¼ cup (90g) honey
⅓ cup (80ml) mild-flavoured extra virgin olive oil
⅓ cup (80ml) milk
1 tablespoon hazelnut-flavoured liqueur

1 Place milk, cream, yolks and sugar in mixing bowl; cook for **8 min/ 90°C/speed** 4 or until well thickened and mixture coats the back of a spoon.
2 Stir in liqueur. Transfer to a large jug and cover surface directly with plastic wrap. Cool to room temperature. Pour mixture equally into two shallow trays. Freeze for 4 hours or overnight until firm.
3 Meanwhile, line an 8cm x 24cm (3¼in x 9½in) loaf pan with two layers of plastic wrap. Store in the freezer until needed.
4 Make chocolate hazelnut spread. Clean mixing bowl. Place hazelnuts, cocoa, vanilla, honey, oil, milk and liqueur in mixing bowl; blend for **10 sec/speed** 7. Scrape down the side of bowl. Blend for **10 sec/speed 10** or until as smooth as possible. Transfer to a small bowl and set aside until needed.
5 Spread half the chocolate hazelnut spread over base of prepared pan. Working quickly so ice-cream doesn't melt, remove one tray from the freezer and use a large metal spoon to chop frozen hazelnut mixture into chunks. Place ice-cream chunks in mixing bowl; blend for **40 sec/speed 8** or until smooth. Spread over the chocolate hazelnut spread layer; cover and freeze for 3 hours or until firm. Repeat with remaining chocolate hazelnut spread and ice-cream. Cover and freeze for 5 hours or overnight until firm.
6 Remove pan from freezer and place in fridge for 20 minutes to soften slightly before turning out onto a platter. Sprinkle with extra chopped hazelnuts and dust with cocoa to serve; cut into slices.

try this Chocolate hazelnut spread, with or without the liqueur, is delicious on toast or as a filling for shortbreads and sponge cakes.

BANANA PEANUT BUTTER CHOC-TOPS

prep + cook time 25 minutes (+ freezing) makes 8

1kg (2lb) ripe bananas, cut into 1cm (½in) slices
¾ cup (210g) smooth peanut butter (see tips)
½ cup (125ml) coconut cream
1 tablespoon pure maple syrup
2 teaspoons vanilla extract
8 waffle ice-cream cones (35g)
300g (9oz) dark chocolate (70% cocoa), broken into chunks
2 tablespoons roasted unsalted peanuts, chopped coarsely

1 Place banana slices in resealable plastic bags; freeze overnight or until completely frozen.
2 Place frozen banana, ½ cup (140g) of the peanut butter, the coconut cream, maple syrup and vanilla in mixing bowl; blend for **30 sec/speed 9** or until finely chopped. Scrape down the side of bowl. Repeat until mixture forms a soft-serve ice-cream texture.
3 Spoon half the ice-cream into a 1-litre (4-cup) freezer-proof container. Drizzle with 2 tablespoons of the peanut butter. Pour remaining ice-cream on top. Drizzle over remaining peanut butter; gently swirl peanut butter through ice-cream. Freeze for 30 minutes or until just firm enough to scoop.
4 Top cones with scoops of ice-cream. Place cones in tall glasses or a cone stand to keep upright. Return to freezer for 10 minutes to firm up.
5 Meanwhile, place chocolate in mixing bowl; chop for **8 sec/speed** 7 or until finely chopped. Scrape down the side of bowl. Cook for **5 min/50°C/ reverse/speed 2**, stopping after 2 minutes to scrape down side of bowl, or until chocolate is melted. Repeat until chocolate is completely melted. Pour into a small wide glass (this will make it easier to dip the ice-creams).
6 Dip ice-creams, one at a time, into melted chocolate; sprinkle with peanuts. Place ice-creams back in glasses and return to the freezer for 5 minutes or until chocolate is set. Serve.

tips We used a natural peanut butter without emulsifiers, which made it easier to drizzle.
Make sure you have space in the freezer to store the ice-creams upright. Choc-tops are best eaten immediately after chocolate has set.

VEGAN LEMON PASSIONFRUIT CHEESECAKE

prep + cook time *35 minutes (+ standing, freezing, cooling & refrigeration)* ***serves*** *16*

- 3 cups (450g) raw cashews (see tips)
- 220g (7oz) cacao butter, chopped
- 1 cup (140g) unsalted macadamias
- ½ cup (60g) pecans
- ⅔ cup (55g) desiccated coconut
- ⅔ cup (160ml) pure maple syrup
- ½ cup (125ml) coconut cream
- 1 tablespoon finely grated lemon rind
- ⅓ cup (80ml) lemon juice
- ¾ teaspoon agar agar powder
- ¼ teaspoon stevia liquid
- ¾ cup passionfruit pulp (180g) (see tips)

1 Place cashews in a medium bowl; cover with cold water. Cover and set aside for 4 hours or overnight. Drain cashews and rinse under cold running water; drain well.

2 Grease a 23cm (9¼in) round springform cake pan; line base and side with baking paper, extending paper 5cm (2in) above side.

3 Place 60g (2oz) of the cacao butter in mixing bowl; cook for **2 min/50°C/reverse/speed 2** or until melted. Add macadamias, pecans, desiccated coconut and 1 tablespoon of the maple syrup; blend for **5 sec/speed 5** or until mixture resembles coarse crumbs. Press mixture over base of pan; use the back of a spoon to press down firmly and smooth surface. Freeze for 15 minutes or until firm.

4 Meanwhile, wash and dry mixing bowl. Place remaining cacao butter in mixing bowl; cook for **3 min/50°C/reverse/speed 2** or until melted. Add half the drained cashews, half the remaining maple syrup, and half each of the coconut cream, lemon rind and juice; blend for **20 sec/speed 10** or until combined. Scrape down the side of bowl. Blend a further **1 min/speed 7** or until smooth. Transfer cashew mixture to a medium bowl and reserve. Repeat with remaining cashews, maple syrup, coconut cream, lemon rind and juice. Return reserved cashew mixture to mixing bowl; blend for **20 sec/speed 10** or until as smooth as possible. Pour mixture over base and smooth top. Freeze for 2 hours or refrigerate overnight until firm.

5 Wash mixing bowl. Place ¾ cup (180g) cold water, agar agar and stevia in mixing bowl; blend for **10 sec/speed 5** or until combined. Scrape down the side of bowl. Heat for **5 min/100°C/reverse/speed 3** or until agar agar dissolves. Add passionfruit; mix for **10 sec/reverse/speed 3** or until combined. Set aside for 10 minutes to cool. Pour over cheesecake layer and refrigerate for 20 minutes or until jelly is firm.

6 Run a knife around the inside edge of the cake pan to loosen the jelly; carefully remove cake from pan. Slice cake to serve.

tips To save time, soak cashews in boiling water for 2 hours. You will need about 10 passionfruit for this recipe.

PEAR & CIDER DUMPLINGS

prep + cook time *45 minutes* ***serves*** *4* ***makes*** *16*

1 teaspoon ground cinnamon
1 medium firm beurre bosc pear (240g), quartered, unpeeled, cored
1¼ cups (190g) self-raising flour
30g (1oz) unsalted butter
¼ cup (90g) golden syrup
1 tablespoon milk

PEAR CIDER SAUCE

2 thick strips orange rind
3 medium firm beurre bosc pears (720g), unpeeled, cut into 6 wedges
2⅔ cups (660ml) pear cider (see tip)
1 cup (220g) caster (superfine) sugar
¼ cup (90g) golden syrup
60g (2oz) unsalted butter

1 To make the dumplings, place cinnamon in mixing bowl; toast for **2 min/120°C/speed 1**. Add pear; blend for **5 sec/speed 5** until finely chopped. Scrape down the side of bowl. Blend a further **5 sec/speed 5**.
2 Add flour, butter, golden syrup and milk; blend for **10 sec/speed 4** or until just combined (do not overwork dough). With wet hands, roll tablespoons of dough into balls. Place balls on lightly greased steaming tray. Stack tray on top of steaming dish, cover and set aside.
3 Make pear cider sauce. Clean mixing bowl. Place all sauce ingredients in mixing bowl; cook for **25 min/steam mode/reverse/stir mode,** checking regularly until boiling (this should take about 7 minutes). Once boiling, position steaming dish and tray over mixing bowl; continue cooking for 18 minutes or until dumplings are cooked through. Transfer pears to a dish and keep warm.
4 Remove steaming dish and tray from mixing bowl; keep warm. Pour the pear sauce into a medium saucepan over high heat; bring to the boil and cook for 12 minutes or until reduced by half. Serve dumplings with pears and pear sauce.

tip You can substitute the pear cider for apple cider or non-alcoholic sparkling apple drink, if you like.
try this Serve with thick (double) cream.

ROSEWATER & MACADAMIA PANNA COTTA

***prep + cook time** 20 minutes (+ standing & refrigeration)*
***serves** 6*

350g (11oz) unsalted macadamias
2½ teaspoons powdered gelatine
300ml pouring cream
1 tablespoon rosewater
2 tablespoons caster (superfine) sugar
½ teaspoon vanilla extract
⅓ cup (50g) pomegranate seeds
1 tablespoon honey
2 small fresh figs (100g), quartered

1 To make macadamia milk, place macadamias in a large bowl and cover with hot water; cover and set aside for 2 hours. Drain; rinse under cold running water. Place drained macadamias and 2 cups (500g) water in mixing bowl; blend for **2 min/speed 10**. Strain through a nut bag or a large clean dish cloth into a medium bowl, squeezing to extract as much liquid as possible (see tips). You will need 300ml milk for this recipe; top up with a little water, milk or cream, if necessary, to make 300ml.
2 Place gelatine and 2 tablespoons water in a small heatproof cup; place cup in a larger bowl of boiling water. Whisk until dissolved.
3 Place cream, rosewater, sugar, vanilla and 300ml macadamia milk in mixing bowl; heat for **4 min/75°C/speed 2**. Add gelatine mixture; heat for **1 min/75°C/speed 2** or until sugar and gelatine are dissolved. Do not boil.
4 Grease six ½ cup (125ml) moulds or ramekins with flavourless oil (see tips). Pour mixture into moulds. Refrigerate for 4 hours or overnight until set.
5 Meanwhile, combine pomegranate seeds, honey and figs in a medium bowl; refrigerate until required.
6 Turn panna cottas out onto plates. Serve with pomegranate mixture.

tips You can also strain the nuts through four layers of muslin.
We used vegetable oil to grease our moulds. Grapeseed oil would be a good option, too.
try this This is a soft-set panna cotta. If you would prefer not to turn the panna cottas out, you can set the mixture into decorative cups or glasses.

STEAMED CHOCOLATE & PISTACHIO CHEESECAKE

***prep + cook time** 1 hour 30 minutes (+ refrigeration)* ***serves** 10*

¾ cup (105g) roasted unsalted shelled pistachios, plus extra coarsely chopped to serve
200g (6½oz) plain sweet biscuits, such as granita
80g (2½oz) butter, melted
¾ cup (165g) raw sugar
200g (6½oz) dark (semi-sweet) chocolate, broken into pieces
1 tablespoon instant coffee granules
500g (1lb) cream cheese, chopped
3 eggs
1 cup (240g) sour cream
125g (4oz) fresh raspberries

1 Line the base and side of a 6.5cm (2¾in) deep, 19cm (7¾in) springform cake pan with baking paper. Place pistachios in mixing bowl; chop for **4 sec/speed 8**. Add biscuits; chop for **5 sec/speed 6** or until fine crumbs. Add butter; mix for **8 sec/reverse/speed 6** or until ingredients clump together. Tip mixture into prepared pan and press firmly over base and all the way up the side. Chill in fridge for 15 minutes.

2 Clean and dry mixing bowl. Place sugar in mixing bowl; grind for **8 sec/speed 9** or until a fine powder. Remove 1 tablespoon of ground sugar and reserve. Add chocolate and coffee to mixing bowl; chop for **8 sec/speed 9** or until finely ground. Cook for **2 min/70°C/speed 3** or until melted and fudge like.

3 Add half the cream cheese to mixing bowl; cook for **1 min/50°C/speed 4.** Add remaining cream cheese; cook for **30 sec/50°C/speed 5** or until well combined. Add eggs and ½ cup of the sour cream; mix for **30 sec/speed 5** or until smooth. Pour into chilled crust. Grease a large sheet of foil and cover pan, folding tightly underneath pan to secure.

4 Clean mixing bowl, then fill with 7 cups (1.75kg) hot water. Place two small jar lids or small dipping bowl in steaming dish. Place cake pan on top. Position covered steaming dish over mixing bowl. Cook for **70 min/steam mode/speed 2** or until cheesecake is set with a slight wobble in the centre. Chill for 4 hours or overnight.

5 Release cheesecake from pan. Combine reserved sugar and remaining sour cream in a small bowl. Serve cheesecake topped with sour cream mixture, fresh raspberries and extra pistachios.

APPLE PIE CRUMBLE

prep + cook time 35 minutes serves 6

8 small green apples (1kg), peeled, quartered, cored
125g (4oz) butter, plus 20g (¾oz) extra
¾ cup (115g) coconut sugar, plus 1 tablespoon extra
2 tablespoons white spelt flour
2 teaspoons ground cinnamon
½ cup (60g) pecans
½ cup (80g) natural almonds
½ cup (45g) rolled oats
2 teaspoons vanilla bean paste
custard or ice-cream, to serve

1 Place apples, butter, coconut sugar, flour, cinnamon and ⅓ cup (80g) water in mixing bowl; cook for **25 min/120°C/reverse/stir mode** or until apples are softened.
2 Preheat grill (broiler) to medium.
3 Transfer apple mixture to a 16cm x 21cm (6½in x 8½in), 1.75 litre (7-cup) ovenproof dish.
4 Place pecans, almonds, oats, vanilla, extra butter and extra sugar in mixing bowl; mix for **4 sec/speed 5** or until coarse crumbs. Scatter evenly over apple mixture.
5 Grill for 6 minutes or until crunchy and bubbling. Serve warm with custard or ice-cream.

try this See our Basic Vanilla Custard and Ice-cream recipe on page 184 for the perfect accompaniment.

TROPICAL RICE PUDDING
WITH BROWN SUGAR SYRUP

prep + cook time 50 minutes serves 4

2 x 400ml cans coconut milk
1 cup (200g) arborio rice, rinsed
2 tablespoons brown sugar
2 teaspoons finely grated lime rind
2 kaffir lime leaves, very finely shredded
½ small pineapple (450g), cut into triangles
⅓ cup (15g) flaked coconut, toasted
½ small red papaya, cut into wedges

BROWN SUGAR SYRUP

½ cup (110g) brown sugar
¼ cup (60ml) lime juice
2 kaffir lime leaves

1 Make brown sugar syrup. Place sugar, ¼ cup (60g) water, lime juice and lime leaves in mixing bowl; cook for **10 min/100°C/stir mode** or until thickened slightly. Transfer to a small jug and refrigerate until required.
2 Clean mixing bowl and insert butterfly whisk. Place coconut milk, rice and ¼ cup (60g) water in mixing bowl; cook for **30 min/90°C/reverse/speed 1.5** or until rice is just tender.
3 Add sugar, lime rind and lime leaf to mixing bowl; mix for **40 sec/reverse/speed 3**.
4 Divide mixture among serving glasses or bowls. Top with pineapple and flaked coconut; drizzle with the sugar syrup. Serve with papaya.

tip Rice pudding mixture will thicken on standing; it can be thinned with a little more coconut milk, milk or water, if necessary.
try this You could use mango instead of the papaya in this recipe.

PLUM & STAR ANISE GELATO

***prep + cook time** 30 minutes (+ freezing)* ***serves** 4*
***makes** 1.25 litres*

2 whole star anise
200g (6½oz) caster (superfine) sugar, plus 1 tablespoon extra
250g (8oz) plums, halved, plus 4 plums extra
1 teaspoon vanilla extract
200g (6½oz) liquid glucose
2 cups (500ml) pouring cream

1 Place star anise and 1 tablespoon of the sugar in mixing bowl; blend for **20 sec/speed 10**. Repeat until star anise is finely ground, if necessary. Add plums and vanilla; blend for **30 sec/speed 10** or until very smooth. Add remaining sugar and glucose; cook for **5 min/80°C/speed 2** or until sugar dissolves. Scrape down the side of bowl. Add cream; blend for **10 sec/speed 3** or until smooth.
2 Pour plum mixture into a large shallow tray; freeze for 4 hours or overnight until firm. Place a 1.5-litre (6-cup) loaf pan in the freezer to chill.
3 Working quickly to prevent gelato melting, use a large metal spoon to chop frozen plum mixture into large chunks. Add gelato chunks to mixing bowl; blend for **40 sec/speed 8** or until smooth. Quickly transfer mixture to chilled loaf pan and cover surface directly with plastic wrap; freeze for 3 hours or until firm.
4 Meanwhile, roast extra plums. Preheat oven to 180°C/350°F. Halve plums. Place halved plums on a baking tray and sprinkle with extra sugar. Bake for 10 minutes or until tender; cool.
5 If gelato is too firm when ready to serve, stand at room temperature for 10 minutes to soften slightly before scooping. Serve scoops of ice-cream with roasted plums.

tip The colour of the gelato will vary according to the variety of plum used.

DARK CHOCOLATE POTS DE CRÈME
WITH RHUBARB

prep + cook time *35 minutes (+ refrigeration)* *serves 4*

1½ cups (375ml) pouring cream
100g (3oz) dark chocolate (70% cocoa), broken into chunks
½ teaspoon vanilla extract
3 egg yolks
2 tablespoons caster (superfine) sugar, plus 1 tablespoon extra
6 stalks rhubarb (370g), cut into 6cm (2½in) pieces
thick (double) cream, to serve

1 Ensure four ½-cup (125ml) ramekins fit level into your steaming dish with steaming tray and lid in place.
2 Place pouring cream, chocolate and vanilla in mixing bowl; cook for 4 **min/90°C/speed 1** or until chocolate is melted and mixture is hot.
3 Add yolks and caster sugar; mix for 4 **sec/speed 5** or until completely smooth. Divide mixture evenly among ramekins; place in steaming dish. Cover all four ramekins tightly with one sheet of foil.
4 Line steaming tray with baking paper; place rhubarb on paper and sprinkle with the extra sugar. Stack tray on top of steaming dish, cover and set aside.
5 Clean mixing bowl, then fill with 2 cups (500g) water; heat for **10 min/ steam mode/speed 2** or until boiling. Position steaming dish and tray over mixing bowl; cook for **10 min/steam mode/speed 1** or until rhubarb is just tender but still holding its shape. Remove steaming tray; keep warm. Return lid to steaming dish; continue cooking for 8 minutes or until pots are puffed slightly and have a slight wobble. Remove steaming dish from mixing bowl, uncover and allow to cool to room temperature for 10 minutes; refrigerate for 2 hours or until chilled and set.
6 Serve pots topped with thick cream and rhubarb.

FIGGY, GINGER STEAMED PUDDING

prep + cook time 2 hours 20 minutes (+ standing) serves 8

- 1⅓ cups (200g) soft dried figs, trimmed
- 1⅓ cups (200g) raisins
- ¾ cup (105g) dried dates
- ¼ cup (60g) glacé ginger
- 100g (3oz) butter, chopped
- ⅔ cup (145g) firmly packed dark brown sugar
- ¾ teaspoon bicarbonate of soda (baking soda)
- ¼ cup (60ml) brandy, plus 2 tablespoons extra
- 2 eggs
- ⅔ cup (100g) plain (all-purpose) flour
- ⅔ cup (100g) self-raising flour
- 2 teaspoons ground ginger
- 1 teaspoon ground cinnamon
- Orange Custard, to serve (see page 184)
- icing (confectioners') sugar and orange zest, to serve

1 Place figs, raisins, dates and ginger in mixing bowl; chop for **6 sec/speed 5** or until coarsely chopped. Add butter, sugar and ⅔ cup (160g) water; cook for **10 min/90°C/reverse/stir mode**. Add bicarb; stir with spatula. Transfer mixture to a large bowl; stir in brandy. Cool for 5 minutes.
2 Meanwhile, grease an 18cm (7¼in) cake pan; line base and side with baking paper. Rinse mixing bowl, then fill with 8 cups (2kg) water; heat for **12 min/steam mode/speed 2** until boiling.
3 Meanwhile, stir eggs into fruit mixture. Sift in combined flours and spices; mix gently to combine. Spoon mixture into prepared pan. Place a circle of lightly greased baking paper directly on top of mixture. Cover entire pan with a sheet of foil, tucking under pan firmly to secure.
4 Place two upturned sauce dishes or jar lids in steaming dish to elevate pudding; place pudding on top. Position covered steaming dish over mixing bowl; cook for **105 min/steam mode/speed 2** or until a skewer inserted into the centre comes out clean. The mixing bowl will need to be topped up with boiling water from the kettle approximately every 45 minutes. Remove steaming dish from mixing bowl and stand for 10 minutes before transferring the pudding to a plate. Drizzle top of pudding with extra brandy. If not serving pudding immediately, cool in pan.
5 Meanwhile, make the orange custard.
6 Dust pudding with icing sugar and sprinkle with orange zest. Serve warm pudding with orange custard.

tip If custard starts to curdle, blend for **10 sec/speed 2** until smooth.
keep Pudding will keep, tightly wrapped in plastic wrap and foil, for 2 months in the fridge. To reheat pudding, wrap tightly in plastic wrap and place in original cake pan; wrap pan tightly in foil. Fill mixing bowl with 4 cups (1kg) water; heat for **10 min/steam mode/speed 2.** Once boiling, place pudding in steaming dish, cover and position over mixing bowl; cook for **20 min/steam mode/speed 2** or until hot. For faster reheating, cut pudding into portions, wrap individually in plastic wrap and foil, then steam.

BAKING

CHICKEN & PUMPKIN PIES

***prep + cook time** 1 hour 50 minutes (+ refrigeration & standing)* ***serves** 4*

1 large onion (200g), halved
3 cloves garlic
60g (2oz) butter, chopped
1 tablespoon fresh thyme leaves
60g (2oz) plain (all-purpose) flour
2 cups (500ml) chicken stock
1kg (2lb) chicken thigh fillets, cut into 2cm (¾in) pieces
600g (1¼lb) butternut pumpkin, cut into 2cm (¾in) pieces
1 egg, beaten lightly

PARSLEY PASTRY

⅓ bunch fresh flat-leaf parsley
2 cups (300g) plain (all-purpose) flour
½ teaspoon salt flakes
125g (4oz) unsalted butter, chopped coarsely
1 egg
1 egg yolk
3 teaspoons iced water, approximately

1 Make parsley pastry. Place parsley and 1½ teaspoons water in mixing bowl; blend for **6 sec/speed** 7 or until a coarse puree. Add remaining pastry ingredients; mix for **20 sec/speed** 4 or until just combined.

2 Transfer dough to a lightly floured surface and shape into a flat disc. Cover with plastic wrap and chill for at least 30 minutes.

3 Meanwhile, clean mixing bowl. Place onion and garlic in mixing bowl; blend for **3 sec/speed** 5 or until coarsely chopped. Add the butter and thyme; cook for **5 min/120°C/reverse/stir mode** or until softened. Add flour; cook for **5 min/100°C/reverse/stir mode**. Add stock; cook for **5 min/120°C/reverse/speed** 2 until thickened. Season. Transfer sauce to a large bowl.

4 Place chicken on lightly oiled steaming tray and pumpkin in steaming dish; season. Stack tray on top of dish, cover and set aside.

5 Rinse mixing bowl, then fill with 5 cups (1.25kg) water; heat for **10 min/steam mode/speed** 2 or until boiling. Position steaming dish and tray over mixing bowl; cook for **20 min/steam mode/speed** 4 or until pumpkin is tender, stirring chicken occasionally to ensure even cooking. Remove pumpkin from steaming dish when cooked and stir into the sauce in bowl. Continue cooking chicken for 5 minutes or until cooked through, then add to sauce. Spread pie filling out on a tray and refrigerate until cool.

6 Preheat oven to 200°C/400°F. Divide cooled pie filling among four 1¾-cup (430ml) pie dishes.

7 Cut pastry into four portions; roll each portion between two sheets of baking paper until large enough to fit each prepared dish. Cover filling with pastry, pressing edges with a fork to seal. Using a sharp knife, cut a small slit in the centre of each pastry lid. Brush tops with beaten egg.

8 Bake for 40 minutes or until pastry is golden. Stand pies for 20 minutes before serving.

tip If the pastry is dry at the end of step 1, add 1 teaspoon extra water.

VEGIE 'SAUSAGE' ROLLS

prep + cook time 1 hour (+ freezing) makes 16

1 cup (90g) rolled oats
1 medium orange sweet potato (400g), cut into 4cm (1½in) pieces
1 small onion (80g), quartered
2 cloves garlic
1 tablespoon extra virgin olive oil
6 flat mushrooms (480g), halved
¼ cup (70g) tomato paste
2 teaspoons ground cumin
1 teaspoon ground cinnamon
2 x 400g (12½oz) cans brown lentils, drained, rinsed
1 egg, beaten lightly
4 sheets frozen puff pastry (495g), just thawed, halved lengthways
2 tablespoons milk
2 tablespoons white sesame seeds
tomato or barbecue sauce, to serve

1 Preheat oven to 200°C/400°F. Line two oven trays with baking paper.

2 Place oats in mixing bowl; mill for **15 sec/speed 9** or until a coarse flour. Transfer to a small bowl. Add sweet potato to mixing bowl; blend for 7 **sec/speed** 5 or until finely chopped. Transfer to a medium bowl.

3 Place onion and garlic in mixing bowl; chop for 5 **sec/speed** 5 or until finely chopped. Scrape down the side of bowl. Add oil; cook for 5 **min/ steam mode/reverse/speed** 1. Add mushrooms; chop **for 8 sec/speed** 4. Cook for **2 min/steam mode/reverse/speed 1**. Add chopped sweet potato, tomato paste, cumin and cinnamon, then season to taste; cook for **8 min/ steam mode/reverse/speed** 2 or until sauce thickens and sweet potato is tender.

4 Add oat flour to mixing bowl; mix for **20 sec/reverse/speed** 5 or until combined. Transfer mixture to a large bowl. Add lentils and stir to combine; season to taste. Cool slightly. Add egg; stir to combine.

5 Spoon one-eighth of the lentil mixture lengthways down each pastry strip. Brush milk along the opposite edge of pastry and roll up to seal. Place on prepared trays, seam-side down. Freeze for 10 minutes or until pastry is firm but not frozen. Cut rolls in half; brush with more milk and sprinkle with sesame seeds.

6 Bake for 30 minutes or until pastry is golden and cooked through. Serve rolls with tomato or barbecue sauce.

keep Uncooked rolls can be frozen, tightly wrapped in plastic wrap, for up to 2 months. Increase cooking time by 15 minutes if cooking from frozen.

GRAPE, TARRAGON & SICILIAN OLIVE FOCACCIA

prep + cook time 40 minutes (+ standing) serves 4

2 teaspoons (7g) dried yeast
1 teaspoon caster (superfine) sugar
2½ cups (375g) plain (all-purpose) flour
½ cup (125ml) extra virgin olive oil
1½ teaspoons salt flakes, plus extra to serve
⅓ cup fresh tarragon leaves
½ small clove garlic
½ cup (90g) pitted green sicilian olives
300g (9½oz) red grapes, cut into small clusters

1 Place yeast, sugar and 1 cup (250g) water in mixing bowl; heat for **2 min/37°C/speed 1** or until starting to foam.
2 Add flour, 2 tablespoons of the oil, the salt and 1 tablespoon torn tarragon leaves; mix for **6 sec/speed 6** or until combined. Knead for **2 min/dough mode** or until smooth and elastic. Transfer to a large greased bowl; cover and stand in a warm place for 45 minutes or until doubled in size.
3 Meanwhile, to make tarragon oil, clean mixing bowl. Place remaining tarragon, garlic and ¼ cup (60ml) of the remaining oil in mixing bowl; blend for **12 sec/speed 9** or until smooth. Transfer to a small bowl, cover and set aside.
4 Place green olives in mixing bowl; blend for **2 sec/speed 4** or until coarsely chopped.
5 Preheat oven to 220°C/425°F. Grease a 25cm x 37cm (10in x 14¾in) baking tray.
6 Tip dough gently onto prepared tray. Without knocking out all the air, lightly press dough with fingertips to edges of tray or until about 1.5cm (¾in) thick. Press grapes and chopped olives lightly into dough. Cover with a clean tea towel and stand in a warm place for 30 minutes to prove slightly.
7 Drizzle focaccia with remaining oil. Bake for 25 minutes or until golden and base sounds hollow when tapped. Drizzle with the tarragon oil and sprinkle with extra salt flakes to serve.

RASPBERRY ALMOND RICOTTA MUFFINS

prep + cook time *55 minutes* *makes* *12*

100g (3oz) raw buckwheat
½ cup (80g) blanched almonds
½ cup (110g) firmly packed brown sugar
½ cup (40g) quinoa flakes
2 teaspoons gluten-free baking powder
40g (1½oz) unsalted butter
¾ cup (180ml) buttermilk
1 egg
1 teaspoon vanilla extract
300g (9½oz) fresh ricotta
200g (6½oz) frozen raspberries
⅓ cup (25g) flaked almonds
¼ cup (55g) demerara sugar

1 Preheat oven to 180°C/350°F. Line a 12-hole (⅓-cup/80ml) muffin pan with paper cases.

2 Place buckwheat in mixing bowl; mill for **30 sec/speed 9** or until a coarse flour. Add blanched almonds; mill a further **20 sec/speed 9** or until a coarse meal. Add sugar, quinoa flakes and baking powder; mix for **10 sec/reverse/speed 3** or until combined. Transfer to a large bowl and set aside.

3 Place butter in mixing bowl; heat for **2 min/70°C/reverse/speed 2** or until melted. Allow to cool for 5 minutes before adding buttermilk, egg and vanilla; mix for **30 sec/speed 4** or until combined.

4 Make a well in the centre of the dry ingredients and add buttermilk mixture; stir with a spatula until ingredients are just combined (do not overmix). Add two-thirds of the ricotta and three-quarters of the raspberries; stir until just combined.

5 Spoon ⅓ cup of the mixture into each muffin case. Top with remaining ricotta and raspberries; scatter over flaked almonds and sprinkle with demerara sugar. Bake for 40 minutes or until golden and a skewer inserted into the centre of one comes out clean. Cool in pan for 5 minutes. Transfer to a wire rack to cool completely.

keep Muffins can be made a day ahead and stored in an airtight container. They are also suitable to freeze.

OAT & SEED ROLLS

prep + cook time *35 minutes (+ standing)* ***makes*** *16*

2 teaspoons (7g) dried yeast
4 cups (600g) bread flour
1 teaspoon sea salt flakes
100g (3oz) rolled oats
50g (1½oz) black chia seeds
30g (1oz) black and white sesame seeds, plus extra to sprinkle
1 tablespoon fennel seeds, plus extra to sprinkle
40g (1½oz) pepitas (pumpkin seed kernels), plus extra to sprinkle
2 tablespoons honey
2 tablespoons extra virgin olive oil
1 tablespoon milk, for brushing

1 Grease a large oven tray.
2 Place all ingredients, except milk, and 2 cups (500g) lukewarm water in mixing bowl; mix for **20 sec/speed 2** until combined. Knead for **3 min/dough mode**. Dough may be sticky at this stage.
3 Transfer dough to a lightly floured surface; divide into 16 pieces and roll into smooth balls. Place balls on oven tray in four rows, just touching. Cover with a tea towel. Set aside in a warm place to prove for 30 minutes or until doubled in size.
4 Meanwhile, preheat oven to 200°C/400°F.
5 Brush rolls with milk and sprinkle with extra seeds and pepitas. Bake for 25 minutes or until golden brown and bases sound hollow when tapped. Cool on tray for 5 minutes. Transfer to a wire rack to cool completely.

tip Rolls are best eaten on day of baking.
keep You can freeze the rolls for up to 2 months.

HUMMINGBIRD CAKE
WITH CREAM CHEESE FROSTING

prep + cook time 1 hour 10 minutes *serves 10*

2 medium carrots (240g), cut into 2cm (¾in) pieces
1 cup (120g) pecans, toasted, plus extra chopped to serve
2 medium bananas (400g), cut into 2cm (¾in) pieces
220g (7oz) can pineapple pieces, drained well
½ cup (110g) brown sugar
½ cup (110g) caster (superfine) sugar
1½ cups (225g) plain (all-purpose) flour
1 teaspoon bicarbonate of soda (baking soda)
1 teaspoon baking powder
1 teaspoon ground cinnamon
½ cup (125ml) light olive oil
2 eggs

CREAM CHEESE FROSTING

375g (12oz) cream cheese, chilled, chopped
½ cup (80g) icing (confectioners') sugar
1½ tablespoons lemon juice
2 teaspoons vanilla bean paste

1 Preheat oven to 180°C/350°F. Grease and line the base and side of a 22cm (8¾in) springform cake pan with baking paper.
2 Place carrot and pecans in mixing bowl; chop for **5 sec/speed 5** until coarsely grated. Scrape down the side of bowl. Add banana and pineapple; chop for **5 sec/speed 5** or until finely chopped. Scrape down the side of bowl.
3 Add sugars, flour, bicarb, baking powder, cinnamon, oil and eggs; mix for **10 sec/reverse/speed 5** until well combined. Pour batter into prepared pan; bake for 50 minutes or until a skewer inserted into the centre comes out clean. Cool in pan for 10 minutes. Transfer to a wire rack to cool completely.
4 Meanwhile, make cream cheese frosting. Clean and dry mixing bowl. Place cream cheese in mixing bowl; mix for **30 sec/speed 4** or until smooth. Add icing sugar, lemon juice and vanilla; mix for **15 sec/speed 4** or until smooth.
5 Spread frosting over cooled cake. Scatter with extra chopped pecans.

keep The iced cake will keep for 3 days in an airtight container. Uniced cake is suitable to freeze.

LEMON BLACKBERRY TEACAKE

***prep + cook time** 1 hour 10 minutes **serves** 8*

½ cup (80g) almond kernels
1 cup (150g) self-raising flour
⅔ cup (120g) semolina flour
185g (6oz) chilled unsalted butter, chopped
1 cup (220g) caster (superfine) sugar
¾ cup (180ml) milk
2 eggs, beaten lightly
2 tablespoons finely grated lemon rind
250g (8oz) blackberries
1½ cups (240g) icing (confectioners') sugar
1½ tablespoons lemon juice

1 Preheat oven to 160°C/325°F. Butter and flour a 22cm (8¾in) (top measurement) bundt pan very well.
2 Place almonds in mixing bowl; mill for **10 sec/speed** 7 or until finely ground. Add flour, semolina, butter and sugar; mix for **10 sec/speed 10** or until combined and crumbly. Add combined milk, egg and rind; mix for **30 sec/speed** 5.
3 Transfer half the mixture to prepared pan; scatter with one-quarter of the blackberries. Top with remaining batter and another quarter of the blackberries. Bake for 50 minutes or until a skewer inserted into the centre comes out clean. Cool in pan for 10 minutes. Turn out onto a wire rack to cool completely.
4 Meanwhile, clean mixing bowl. Place icing sugar, lemon juice and 10g (½oz) of the remaining blackberries in mixing bowl; mix for **10 sec/speed 9** or until combined and a pouring consistency. Drizzle over cooled cake and top with remaining blackberries.

CASHEW CARAMEL & BANANA CROSTATA

prep + cook time 55 minutes serves 8

1¾ cups (265g) plain (all-purpose) flour
160g (5oz) chilled butter, chopped
2 tablespoons cacao powder, plus extra to serve
1 tablespoon icing (confectioners') sugar
2 egg yolks
2 cups (460g) fresh dates, pitted
1 cup (150g) raw cashews, plus ⅓ cup extra
2 teaspoons vanilla bean paste
1 teaspoon sea salt flakes
4 small bananas (520g), halved lengthways
2 teaspoons lemon juice
⅓ cup (80ml) pure maple syrup

1 Preheat oven to 180°C/350°F.
2 Place flour, butter, cacao powder, icing sugar, egg yolks and 2 tablespoons chilled water in mixing bowl; mix for **4 sec/speed 4** to just combine. Scrape down the side of bowl. Mix for a further **10 sec/speed 6** or until dough just comes together. Transfer to a clean surface. Shape dough into a flat oval. Wrap in plastic wrap and refrigerate for 30 minutes.
3 Meanwhile, wipe mixing bowl clean. Place dates, cashews, vanilla, salt and ⅓ cup (80g) water in mixing bowl; blend for **1 min/speed 5** or until thick and combined. Scrape down the side of bowl. Mix for **10 sec/speed 8** or until almost smooth; some cashew pieces will still be visible. Scrape down the side of bowl.
4 Place pastry onto a large sheet of baking paper. Roll out to a 30cm x 26cm (12in x 10½in) oval. Slide paper and pastry onto a large baking tray. Spread 1⅓ cups of date mixture onto pastry, leaving a 2.5cm (1in) border. Brush banana with lemon juice; arrange on top of date mixture, cut-side up. Using the paper as a guide, fold up the edges of pastry to make a border. Bake for 30 minutes.
5 Meanwhile, add 2 tablespoons of the maple syrup and ¼ cup (60g) water to remaining date mixture in mixing bowl; mix for **10 sec/speed 6** or until smooth. Transfer to a small bowl and set aside for serving.
6 Brush banana on crostata with remaining maple syrup; scatter with extra cashews. Return to the oven for 10 minutes or until banana and cashews are golden and pastry is crisp.
7 Sprinkle extra cacao powder over crostata and serve with remaining date mixture and ice-cream, if you like.

try this For a luscious accompaniment, stir leftover date mixture through coconut yoghurt.

ANYTHING GOES BREAKFAST LOAVES

prep + cook time 45 *minutes* *makes* 8

2¾ cups (245g) rolled oats
⅓ cup (65g) linseeds (flaxseeds)
1 cup (160g) wholemeal self-raising flour
2 teaspoons ground cinnamon
1 teaspoon bicarbonate of soda (baking soda)
1 large green apple (200g), unpeeled, quartered, cored
1½ cups (420g) greek yoghurt
2 eggs
1 teaspoon vanilla extract
2 tablespoons olive oil
⅔ cup (120g) honey, plus extra to serve
1½ cups sliced fruit of choice, such as bananas, plums, apples, pears or berries (see tips)

1 Preheat oven to 180°C/350°F. Grease eight ¾-cup (180ml) holes of a mini loaf pan. Line each hole with a strip of baking paper, extending paper 2cm (¾in) above long sides. Line short sides with smaller pieces of paper.
2 Place 2½ cups of the oats, the seeds and a pinch of salt in mixing bowl; mill for **30 sec/speed 9** or until a fine flour. Add flour, 1 teaspoon of the cinnamon and the bicarb; mix for **5 sec/speed 5** to combine.
3 Add apple to mixing bowl; chop for **5 sec/speed** 7. Add yoghurt, eggs, vanilla, oil and ½ cup of the honey; mix for **90 sec/reverse/speed 3** or until well combined.
4 Divide the mixture between prepared loaf pans. Scatter evenly with fruit of choice; sprinkle with remaining oats and cinnamon. Drizzle remaining honey evenly over loaves. Bake for 30 minutes or until a skewer inserted into the centre of one comes out clean. Cool in pans for 10 minutes, then lift out using the baking paper; transfer to a wire rack to cool completely. Serve drizzled with extra honey, if you like.

tips These easy loaves will work with just about any fruit you have on hand. We used plums, raspberries, blueberries and banana. Small berries can be left whole. Hard fruits such as apples or pears will need to be finely chopped. If using banana, toss in a little lemon juice to prevent browning. Loaves are best eaten on day of baking.
keep Loaves are suitable to freeze for up to 2 months.

CHUNKY DARK CHOCOLATE & COCONUT COOKIES

prep + cook time 25 minutes *makes* 18

180g (5½oz) unsalted butter, softened
¾ cup (165g) brown sugar
1 teaspoon vanilla extract
2 eggs
1⅔ cups (250g) plain (all-purpose) flour
1 teaspoon baking powder
1 cup (90g) rolled oats
1 cup (50g) flaked coconut
½ cup (65g) dried sour cherries or dried cranberries
100g (3oz) dark chocolate (70% cocoa), chopped coarsely (see tip)

1 Preheat oven to 190°C/375°F. Line two large oven trays with baking paper.
2 Place butter, sugar and vanilla in mixing bowl; mix for **1 min/speed** 4. Add 1 egg; mix for **15 sec/speed** 4. Repeat with remaining egg. Scrape down the side of bowl.
3 Add flour, baking powder, half the oats and half the coconut; mix for **30 sec/dough mode**. Add sour cherries, chocolate, remaining oats and coconut; mix for **20 sec/reverse/stir mode** or until combined.
4 Roll 2 tablespoons of mixture into balls; place on baking trays and flatten slightly. Bake for 15 minutes, swapping trays halfway through cooking time, or until golden and cooked through. Cool on trays.

tip You could use white or milk chocolate instead of dark chocolate.
keep Once cool, store cookies in an airtight container for up to 2 weeks.

WHITE CHOCOLATE & CORIANDER MANDARIN CAKE

***prep + cook time** 2 hours* ***serves** 8*

250g (8oz) mandarins, unpeeled (see tip)
270g (8½oz) natural almonds
150g (4½oz) good-quality white chocolate, chopped
2 teaspoons coriander seeds
1 cup (220g) caster (superfine) sugar
50g (1½oz) unsalted butter, softened
4 eggs
1½ teaspoons baking powder

MANDARIN SYRUP

2 tablespoons coriander seeds
1 cup (250ml) mandarin juice
½ cup (180g) honey
3 medium mandarins (600g), peeled, sliced thickly into rounds

1 Preheat oven to 160°C/325°F. Grease and line the base and side of a 20cm (8in) round cake pan with a double layer of baking paper.
2 Place mandarins in mixing bowl and add enough water to cover; cook for **30 min/120°C/reverse/stir mode**. Drain. When cool enough to handle, halve mandarins and remove seeds, if necessary. Return mandarins to mixing bowl; blend for **20 sec/speed 8** or until smooth. Transfer to a medium bowl and set aside.
3 Clean mixing bowl and rinse under cold running water to cool; dry thoroughly. Place almonds and white chocolate in mixing bowl; blend for **12 sec/speed 10** or until very finely ground. Transfer to a medium bowl and set aside.
4 Place coriander seeds in mixing bowl; toast for **2 min/120°C/speed 1**. Add sugar; blend for **20 sec/speed 6** or until finely ground. Add butter, eggs and the mandarin puree; blend for **10 sec/speed 8** or until well combined. Add white chocolate mixture and baking powder; mix for **20 sec/reverse/speed 3** or until combined.
5 Pour mixture into prepared pan; bake for 1 hour 20 minutes or until a skewer inserted into the centre comes out clean. Stand in pan for 10 minutes. Turn out, top-side up, onto a wire rack to cool.
6 Meanwhile, make mandarin syrup. Clean and dry mixing bowl. Place coriander seeds in mixing bowl; toast for **2 min/120°C/speed 1**. Blend for **10 sec/speed 6** or until coarsely ground. Transfer to a small bowl. Place mandarin juice in mixing bowl; cook for **8 min/120°C/speed 1**, without measuring cup inserted into lid, or until reduced by half. Add honey and ground coriander; cook for **2 min/120°C/speed 1** or until thickened. Place sliced mandarins in a medium heatproof bowl; pour syrup over mandarins. Cover and refrigerate until serving.
7 Top cooled cake with sliced mandarins and drizzle with mandarin syrup; serve.

tip You will need about 6 mandarins in total for this recipe.
try this Serve with greek yoghurt.

BAKED PUMPKIN DOUGHNUTS

prep + cook time 1 hour (+ refrigeration) *makes 18*

- 1 cup (80g) desiccated coconut
- 1 cup (150g) coconut sugar
- 1½ cups (200g) gluten-free plain (all-purpose) flour
- 2 teaspoons bicarbonate of soda (baking soda)
- 1½ teaspoons ground cinnamon
- 1½ teaspoons ground ginger
- ½ teaspoon ground nutmeg
- ¼ teaspoon fine salt
- 500g (1lb) jap pumpkin, cut into 3cm (1¼in) pieces
- ½ cup (125ml) coconut cream
- ¼ cup (60ml) extra virgin olive oil
- 2 eggs
- 270g (8½oz) gluten-free caramel chocolate
- 2 tablespoons dried rose petals
- 2 tablespoons cacao nibs

1 Preheat oven to 180°C/350°F. Grease three 6-hole (¼-cup/60ml) silicone or non-stick doughnut pans.

2 Place desiccated coconut in mixing bowl; mill for **30 sec/speed 9** or until the consistency of coarse flour. Scrape down the side of bowl. Add coconut sugar; mill for **15 sec/speed 9** or until powdered. Add flour, bicarb, spices and salt; mix for **15 sec/speed 9**. Transfer dry ingredients to a large bowl and set aside.

3 Fill mixing bowl with 2 cups (500g) water. Add pumpkin to steaming dish, cover and position over mixing bowl; steam for **15 min/steam mode/speed 3** or until pumpkin is soft. Transfer pumpkin to a tray lined with paper towel; set aside for 10 minutes to drain and cool.

4 Dry mixing bowl. Place pumpkin in mixing bowl; blend for **10 sec/speed 6** or until pureed. Scrape down the side of bowl. Add coconut cream, oil and eggs; blend for **30 sec/reverse/speed 4** or until combined. Pour over dry ingredients and mix to combine.

5 Spoon ¼ cup mixture into each prepared doughnut hole. Bake for 20 minutes or until a skewer inserted into the centre of one comes out clean. Cool in pans for 5 minutes. Transfer to a wire rack to cool completely.

6 Meanwhile, clean mixing bowl. Place caramel chocolate in mixing bowl; chop for **4 sec/speed 7** or until finely chopped. Heat for **5 min/50°C/reverse/speed 2** or until chocolate is melted, stopping after 2 minutes to scrape down the side of bowl. Repeat until chocolate is completely melted. Pour melted chocolate into a small bowl and set aside for 10 minutes or until it thickens slightly. Dip doughnuts, one at a time, into melted chocolate; shake off excess. Place on a baking-paper-lined tray. Refrigerate for 10 minutes or until chocolate is set. Repeat dipping doughnuts in a second coat of chocolate. If chocolate has set, heat in microwave on MEDIUM for 10 seconds or until melted and smooth. Decorate with rose petals and/or cacao nibs. Return to fridge for 5 minutes or until chocolate is set.

keep Doughnuts can be made 3 days ahead and stored in an airtight container. Once glazed, store doughnuts in the fridge for up to 3 days. Uniced doughnuts are suitable to freeze for up to 2 months.

CHOCOLATE FUDGE CAKE
WITH SOUR CHERRY BUTTER CREAM

***prep + cook time** 1 hour 45 minutes* ***serves** 12*

360g (11½oz) dark chocolate (70% cocoa), broken into pieces
250g (8oz) butter, chopped
3 eggs
1 cup (220g) dark brown sugar
250g (8oz) sour cream
2 cups (240g) almond meal
1 cup (150g) self-raising flour
½ cup (115g) pitted bottled sour cherries, drained, juice reserved
200g (6½oz) unsalted butter, softened, chopped
2½ cups (400g) icing (confectioners') sugar
cacao nibs and fresh cherries, to serve

1 Preheat oven to 180°C/350°F. Grease and line base and side of a 20cm (8in) round cake pan with baking paper, extending paper 5cm (2in) above side.
2 Place chocolate in mixing bowl; chop for **5 sec/speed 6** or until coarsely chopped. Add butter; heat for **6 min/90°C/speed 0.5** or until melted and smooth.
3 Insert whisk attachment in mixing bowl. Add eggs and sugar; whisk for **5 sec/speed 4** or until smooth. Scrape down the side of bowl. Add sour cream, almond meal, flour and ½ cup (125ml) reserved cherry juice. Whisk for **5 sec/speed 4** or until smooth. Scrape down the side of bowl.
4 Pour batter into prepared pan. Bake for 50 minutes, then cover with foil and bake a further 30 minutes or until cake is risen, cracked slightly and a skewer inserted into the centre comes out with moist crumbs attached. Cake will be slightly soft-set but will firm on cooling. Leave to cool completely in the pan, covered with foil.
5 To make sour cherry buttercream, clean mixing bowl. Place butter and sour cherries in mixing bowl; mix for **20 sec/speed 5** or until butter is smooth and cherries are finely chopped. Insert whisk attachment. Add icing sugar; whisk for **1 min/speed 5** until very light and fluffy, scraping down the side of bowl halfway through whisking. Spread icing evenly over cooled cake; sprinkle with cacao nibs. Serve with fresh cherries.

keep This deliciously fudgy cake will keep for 3 days in an airtight container. For longer periods, it is best to store cake in the fridge; bring to room temperature before serving.

STAPLES

BASIC BREAD DOUGH

***prep + cook time** 30 minutes (+ standing)*
***makes** 2 pizzas or 1 loaf of bread*

2 cups (300g) bread flour
½ cup (80g) semolina flour (see tip)
2 teaspoons sea salt flakes
1 cup (250ml) lukewarm water
2 teaspoons (7g) dried yeast
1 tablespoon olive oil

1 Place flours, salt, the water, yeast and oil in mixing bowl; blend for **20 sec/speed 2** to combine. Knead for **3 min/dough mode**. Turn dough out onto a lightly floured surface and shape into a ball. Place in a large oiled bowl, cover and set aside in a warm place for 1½ hours or until doubled in size.
2 Preheat oven to 220°C/425°F.
3 To make pizza, follow recipe on page 96. To make bread, turn dough out onto a lightly floured surface. Without knocking out the air, gently roll dough into a 22.5cm (9in) log. Transfer to a greased baking tray, cover with plastic wrap and set aside in a warm place for 1 hour or until almost doubled in size.
4 Using a very sharp thin-bladed knife or razor blade, make 3–4 shallow cuts diagonally on top of loaf. Bake loaf for 24 minutes or until browned and loaf sounds hollow when tapped. Cool on tray.

tip If you can't find semolina flour, replace with coarse semolina and mill in mixing bowl for **10 sec/speed 10** or until a fine flour.

BÉCHAMEL SAUCE

prep + cook time 11–15 *minutes* ***makes*** *1 litre*

100g (3oz) unsalted butter
⅔ cup (100g) plain (all-purpose) flour
1 litre (4 cups) milk

CHEESE SAUCE

120g (4oz) cheddar cheese, cut into 3cm (1¼in) cubes
40g (1½oz) parmesan, cut into 3cm (1¼in) cubes
¼ teaspoon ground nutmeg

SPINACH & HERB

100g (3oz) baby spinach leaves
1 tablespoon fresh thyme leaves
½ cup fresh flat-leaf parsley leaves

SWEET VANILLA SPICE

1 teaspoon vanilla bean paste
½ teaspoon ground cinnamon
¼ teaspoon ground cardamom
¼ cup (55g) caster (superfine) sugar

1 Place butter, flour and milk in mixing bowl; cook for **11 min/90°C/speed 4** or until thickened. Season with salt and pepper.

CHEESE SAUCE

Add cheeses and nutmeg to mixing bowl along with base recipe ingredients; cook for **13 min/90°C/speed 4**. Season with salt and pepper.

SPINACH & HERB

Add spinach, thyme and parsley to mixing bowl along with base recipe ingredients; cook for **13 min/90°C/speed 4**. Season with salt and pepper.

SWEET VANILLA SPICE

Add vanilla, cinnamon, cardamom and sugar to mixing bowl along with base recipe ingredients; cook for **11 min/90°C/speed 4**. If a thinner sauce is preferred, thin with a little milk or cream until the desired consistency is reached.

try this The cheese sauce is delicious in a vegetable bake or lasagne, the spinach and herb sauce goes well with poached or roasted chicken or fish, while the sweet vanilla spice béchamel is delicious with poached fruit or with puddings instead of custard.

MASHED POTATO/ SWEET POTATO

prep + cook time 30–40 minutes serves 6

MASHED POTATO

1kg (2lb) desiree potatoes or orange sweet potatoes, cut into 3cm (1¼in) pieces
1 teaspoon salt flakes
1 cup (250ml) milk
30g (1oz) butter
olive oil, to serve

ROOT VEGETABLE MASH

400g (12½oz) carrots, cut into 3cm (1¼in) pieces (see tip)
600g (1¼lb) parsnips, cut into 4cm (1½in) pieces (see tip)
75g (2½oz) butter, chopped coarsely

MASHED POTATO

1 Insert whisk into mixing bowl. Place potatoes, salt and milk in mixing bowl; cook for **25 min/95°C/speed 1** or until potato is tender. Add butter; mix for **30 sec/speed 3** or until smooth. Season to taste with salt and pepper. Drizzle with olive oil to serve.

ROOT VEGETABLE MASH

1 Fill mixing bowl with 2 cups (500g) water. Place vegetables in steaming basket and insert into mixing bowl; cook for **35 min/steam mode/ speed 3** or until very tender. Stir vegetables halfway through cooking time to ensure even cooking.
2 Discard water in mixing bowl. Place cooked vegetables, butter, and salt and pepper to taste in mixing bowl; blend for **20 sec/speed 5** or until a coarse puree. Repeat for a smoother consistency.

tip To mix it up, try using celeriac or swede.

ml 500
400
300
200
100

DAIRY-FREE
NUT MILKS

***prep time** 10 minutes (+ standing)* ***makes** 300ml*

2½ cups macadamias, almonds, cashews, hazelnuts or pecans
25cm (10in) piece muslin

1 Place nuts in a large bowl and cover with hot water. Cover and stand for 2 hours for macadamias and 4 hours for other nuts, or overnight, if you have time.
2 Drain and rinse nuts under cold running water; drain well. Place nuts and 2 cups (500g) water in mixing bowl; blend for **2 min/speed 10** or until very smooth.
3 Place a medium sieve over a medium bowl and line with muslin (or a nut bag). Strain milk through muslin, squeezing cloth to extract as much liquid as possible. Place milk in a glass jar and refrigerate.

try this Save the nut pulp and dry it out in a slow oven to use for cereal toppings or to add to curries and pastes.
To make coconut milk, substitute nuts for desiccated coconut and soak in very hot water for 1 hour; strain. Blend for **1 min/speed 10**. Continue with step 3.
keep Refrigerate nut milk for up to 5 days.

VEGIE-PACKED FLAVOUR BOOSTS

prep + cook time 30 minutes ***makes** 2 cups each flavour*

1 medium onion (150g), quartered
2 cloves garlic
2 tablespoons extra virgin olive oil
1 tablespoon sea salt flakes

RED VEG

1 small red capsicum (bell pepper) (150g), seeded, chopped
2 teaspoons fresh thyme leaves
400g (12½oz) can diced tomatoes
pinch caster (superfine) sugar

ORANGE VEG

2 medium carrots (240g), cut into 4cm (1½in) pieces
350g (11oz) butternut pumpkin, cut into 4cm (1½in) pieces
1 tablespoon chopped fresh rosemary

GREEN VEG

1 medium zucchini (120g), cut into 5cm (2in) pieces
200g (6½oz) trimmed broccoli, cut into florets
1 tablespoon fresh thyme leaves
60g (2oz) baby spinach leaves

WHITE VEG

1 large leek (500g), trimmed, cut into 4cm (1½in) lengths
1 medium fennel bulb (300g), trimmed, quartered, fronds reserved
2 teaspoons fennel seeds
2 teaspoons fresh lemon thyme leaves

1 Place onion and garlic in mixing bowl; chop for 5 **sec/speed** 5. Add oil and salt; cook for 5 **min/steam mode/reverse/stir mode**.

RED VEG

1 Follow step 1 of base recipe. Add capsicum and thyme to mixing bowl; chop for 5 **sec/speed** 5. Cook for 5 **min/steam mode/reverse/speed** 1. Add tomatoes, sugar and pepper to taste; cook for 15 **min/100°C/reverse/speed 1**, with simmering basket in place of measuring cup, or until thickened. Season with pepper. Cool slightly.
2 Insert measuring cup into lid. Blend for 15 **sec/speed** 5 or until smooth. Spoon mixture into ice-cube trays. Freeze for 4 hours or overnight until firm.

ORANGE VEG

1 Follow step 1 of base recipe. Add carrot, pumpkin and rosemary to mixing bowl; chop for **8 sec/speed 6**. Cook for 15 **min/100°C/reverse/speed** 1, without measuring cup inserted into lid, or until very tender. Season with pepper. Cool slightly.
2 Insert measuring cup into lid. Blend for 15 **sec/speed** 5 or until smooth. Spoon mixture into ice-cube trays. Freeze for 4 hours or overnight until firm.

GREEN VEG

1 Follow step 1 of base recipe. Add zucchini, broccoli and thyme to mixing bowl; chop for **8 sec/speed** 5. Cook for **10 min/steam mode/reverse/speed** 1, without measuring cup inserted into lid, or until tender. Add spinach; cook for 4 **min/ 100°C/reverse/speed** 1 or until wilted. Season with pepper. Cool slightly.
2 Insert measuring cup into lid. Blend for 15 **sec/speed** 5 or until smooth. Spoon mixture into ice-cube trays. Freeze for 4 hours or overnight until firm.

WHITE VEG

1 Follow step 1 of base recipe. Add leek, fennel, fennel seeds and thyme to mixing bowl; cook for 5 **min/steam mode/reverse/speed** 1. Remove measuring cup from lid. Cook for **10 min/100°C/reverse/speed** 1 or until tender. Season with pepper.
2 Cool slightly. Insert measuring cup into lid. Blend for 15 **sec/speed** 5 or until smooth. Stir in 1 tablespoon reserved chopped fennel fronds. Spoon mixture into ice-cube trays. Freeze for 4 hours or overnight until firm.

tip Frozen cubes can be released from trays and stored in resealable plastic bags.
try this For a quick pasta sauce, place 2 flavour cubes in a small saucepan over low-medium heat. Add 1½ cups cooked pasta and 1 tablespoon extra virgin olive oil; stir over heat until melted. To this base you can add halved cherry tomatoes, baby spinach leaves, basil leaves, grated parmesan, prosciutto, olives and so on. For a flavourful broth, dissolve 2 flavour cubes in 1 cup (250ml) boiling water. For a burst of flavour in meals, drop 1–2 cubes into soups, sauces and stews.

FOWLERS
use by
10/10/20

TOMATO PASSATA

prep + cook time 1 hour makes 1.5 litres

2 medium onions (300g), quartered
4 cloves garlic
¼ cup (60ml) olive oil
1 tablespoon thyme leaves
1.5kg (3lb) very ripe roma tomatoes, cored, quartered (see tip)
2 teaspoons salt flakes
1 teaspoon sugar

1 Place onion and garlic in mixing bowl; chop for 5 **sec/speed** 5. Scrape down the side of bowl.
2 Add oil and thyme; cook for **8 min/120°C/speed 1** without measuring cup inserted into lid.
3 Add tomatoes, salt and sugar; blend for **10 sec/speed** 5. Cook for **45 min/100°C/speed 2**, with simmering basket in place of measuring cup, or until thickened. Insert measuring cup into lid. Blend for **20 sec/speed** 9 or until very smooth. Check the seasoning and adjust with a little more salt or sugar, if necessary.

tip To get the best-flavoured passata, store your tomatoes at room temperature until very ripe.
keep Passata can be stored in an airtight container in the fridge for up to 1 week or frozen for 2 months. For longer periods, store in sealed sterilised jars (see page 194) in a cool, dark place.
try this Passata can be used as a pasta or pizza sauce, or anywhere you would use canned diced tomatoes.

BASIC VANILLA CUSTARD & ICE-CREAM

***prep + cook time** 10–15 minutes (+ refrigeration & freezing)*
***makes** 3 cups*

110g (3½oz) caster (superfine) sugar
7 egg yolks
1 teaspoon vanilla bean paste
600ml pouring cream

CUSTARD

Place all ingredients in mixing bowl; cook for **8 min/90°C/speed** 4 or until thick. Blend for **10 sec/speed 5**. Immediately transfer to a bowl or jug to cool, as residual heat may cause custard to overcook. Cover surface directly with plastic wrap and refrigerate until chilled.

ICE-CREAM

To make ice-cream, pour custard into a shallow metal tray; freeze for 4 hours or overnight until completely frozen. Place a 1-litre (4-cup) loaf pan in the freezer to chill. Working quickly, break up frozen custard with a large metal spoon. Place custard chunks in mixing bowl; blend for **40 sec/speed 8** or until smooth. Transfer to chilled loaf pan. Freeze for 1–2 hours or until just firm.

VARIATIONS

cinnamon custard or ice-cream Replace the vanilla with ½ teaspoon ground cinnamon.

orange custard or ice-cream Use a vegetable peeler to remove the rind from half an orange, avoiding the white pith. Place rind and sugar in mixing bowl; chop for **10 sec/speed 10** or until finely chopped. Add remaining ingredients and continue with custard recipe, stirring in 2 tablespoons orange-flavoured liqueur at the end. Continue with ice-cream recipe to make orange ice-cream.

pyrex

ANY BERRY JAM

***prep + cook time** 30 minutes* ***makes** 1 litre*

500g (1lb) frozen raspberries, thawed (see tips)
125g (4oz) frozen blueberries, thawed
125g (4oz) frozen strawberries, thawed
¼ cup (60ml) lemon juice
3¼ cups (715g) white granulated sugar

1 Place all ingredients in mixing bowl; blend for **5 sec/speed 3**. Scrape down the side of bowl.
2 Cook for **25 min/steam mode/speed 1**, with simmering basket in place of measuring cup, scraping down side after 5 minutes, or until jam reaches setting point (see tips). Pour mixture into hot sterilised jars (see page 194) and seal immediately.

tips Use any combination of berries to the equivalent of 750g (1½lb). To test whether jam is ready, place a saucer in the freezer. Drop a teaspoon of jam onto the cold saucer and return to the freezer for 1 minute. Gently push jam with your finger: if it wrinkles and is thickened, it is ready; if not, cook the jam for 2 more minutes and test again.

PEANUT BUTTER

***prep time** 5 minutes **makes** 1½ cups*

280g (9oz) roasted salted peanuts (see tips)
1 tablespoon olive oil
1 teaspoon honey

1 Place peanuts in mixing bowl; chop for **10 sec/speed 4.5** or until coarsely chopped. For a crunchy peanut butter, remove one-third of the peanuts and reserve. Add oil and honey to mixing bowl; blend for **30 sec/speed 9,** scraping down side occasionally if necessary, or until smooth. Return chopped peanuts to mixing bowl; mix for **5 sec/reverse/stir mode** or until combined.
2 Spoon peanut butter into a jar and refrigerate. Stir before using, as the oil will settle on top.

tips Use unsalted nuts for a healthier peanut butter, if you like. For a different nut butter, try swapping the peanuts with cashews or macadamias.
try this Serve with some crusty bread.

GLOSSARY

ALLSPICE so-named because it tastes like a combination of nutmeg, cumin, clove and cinnamon. Available whole or ground.

ALMONDS

blanched brown skins removed from the kernel.

flaked paper-thin slices of blanched or natural almonds.

meal also known as ground almonds; powdered to a coarse flour-like texture.

natural almond kernels with the brown skin on.

slivered small pieces cut lengthways.

ANCHOVIES small oily fish. Anchovy fillets are preserved and packed in oil or salt in small cans or jars, and are strong in flavour. Fresh anchovies are much milder in flavour.

BAKING POWDER a raising agent consisting mainly of two parts cream of tartar to one part bicarbonate of soda.

BARLEY a nutritious grain used in soups and stews. Hulled barley, the least processed, is high in fibre. Pearl barley has had the husk removed then steamed and polished so that only the "pearl" of the original grain remains, much the same as white rice.

BEANS

black also called turtle beans or black kidney beans; an earthy-flavoured dried bean completely different from the better-known Chinese black beans (fermented soy beans). Used mostly in Mexican and South American cooking.

borlotti also called roman beans or pink beans, can be eaten fresh or dried. Interchangeable with pinto beans due to their similarity in appearance – pale pink or beige with dark red streaks.

broad (fava) available dried, fresh, canned and frozen. Fresh should be peeled twice (discarding the outer long green pod and the beige-green tough inner shell); frozen beans have had their pods removed but the beige shell still needs removal.

butter a large beige bean having a mealy texture and mild taste. Cans labelled butter beans are, in fact, cannellini beans. Confusingly butter is also another name for lima beans (dried and canned).

green also known as french or string beans (although the tough string they once had has generally been bred out of them), this long thin fresh bean is consumed in its entirety once cooked.

BICARBONATE OF SODA [BAKING SODA] a raising agent.

BREADCRUMBS, PANKO [JAPANESE] are available in two kinds: larger pieces and fine crumbs; have a lighter texture than Western-style ones. Available from Asian food stores and most supermarkets.

BROCCOLINI a cross between broccoli and chinese kale, it has long asparagus-like stems with a long loose floret; both are edible. Resembles broccoli but is milder and sweeter in taste.

BUCKWHEAT a herb in the same plant family as rhubarb, so it is gluten free. Available as flour, ground (cracked) into coarse, medium or fine granules (kasha) and used similarly to polenta; or groats, the whole kernel sold roasted as a cereal product.

BURGHUL also called bulgar wheat; hulled steamed wheat kernels that, once dried, are crushed into various sized grains. Used in Middle Eastern dishes such as falafel, kibbeh and tabbouleh. Is not the same as cracked wheat.

BUTTERMILK originally the term given to the slightly sour liquid left after butter was churned from cream, today it is made from no-fat or low-fat milk to which specific bacterial cultures have been added.

CAPERS grey-green buds of a warm climate shrub (usually Mediterranean); sold dried and salted or pickled in a vinegar brine. Rinse before using.

CARDAMOM a spice native to India and used extensively in its cuisine; can be purchased in pod, seed or ground form. Has a distinctive aromatic, sweetly rich flavour.

CAVOLO NERO [TUSCAN CABBAGE] it has long, narrow, wrinkled leaves and a rich and astringent, mild cabbage flavour. It doesn't lose its volume like silver beet or spinach when cooked, but it does need longer cooking.

CHEESE

cream commonly called Philadelphia or philly; a soft cow-milk cheese, its fat content ranges from 14–33%.

fetta Greek in origin; a crumbly textured goat- or sheep-milk cheese with a sharp, salty taste. Ripened and stored in salted whey.
goat's made from goat's milk, has an earthy, strong taste; available in both soft and firm textures, in various shapes and sizes, and sometimes rolled in ash or herbs.
haloumi a firm, cream-coloured sheep-milk cheese matured in brine. Haloumi can be grilled or fried, briefly, without breaking down; should be eaten while still warm as it becomes tough and rubbery on cooling.
mozzarella soft, spun-curd cheese, originating in southern Italy where it was traditionally made from water-buffalo milk. Now generally made from cow's milk, it is the most popular pizza cheese because of its low melting point and elasticity when heated.
parmesan also called parmigiano; traditional Italian parmesan is a hard, grainy cow-milk cheese made from calves rennet. You can find vegetarian versions of parmesan-style cheese made with vegetable or microbial-based rennet; when purchasing, check the ingredients to see the brand you buy is in fact suitable for vegetarians.
pecorino the Italian generic name for cheeses made from sheep milk; hard, white to pale-yellow in colour. If you can't find it, use parmesan instead.
pizza cheese a commercial blend of processed grated mozzarella, cheddar and parmesan cheeses.
ricotta a soft, sweet, moist, white cow-milk cheese with a low fat content and a slightly grainy texture. The name roughly translates as 'cooked again' and refers to ricotta's manufacture from a whey that is itself a by-product of other cheese making.
CHIA SEEDS contain protein and all the essential amino acids and a wealth of vitamins, minerals and antioxidants, as well as being fibre rich.
CHICKPEAS [GARBANZO BEANS] an irregularly round, sandy-coloured legume. Has a firm texture even after cooking, a floury mouth-feel and robust nutty flavour; available canned or dried (soak for several hours in cold water before use).
CHILLI available in many types and sizes. Use rubber gloves when seeding and chopping fresh chillies as they can burn your skin. Removing membranes and seeds lessens the heat level.
flakes dried, deep-red, dehydrated chilli slices with seeds.
green any unripened chilli; also some particular varieties that are ripe when green, such as jalapeño, habanero, poblano or serrano.
long red available fresh and dried; a generic term used for any moderately hot, thin, long chilli.
CHINESE COOKING WINE [SHAO HSING] also called chinese rice wine; made from fermented rice, wheat, sugar and salt. Found in Asian food shops; if you can't find it, use mirin or sherry.
CHOCOLATE
dark (semi-sweet) also called luxury chocolate; made of a high percentage of cocoa liquor and cocoa butter, and little added sugar.
white contains no cocoa solids but derives its sweet flavour from cocoa butter. It is very sensitive to heat.
CHOY SUM a member of the buk choy family; easy to identify with its long stems, light green leaves and yellow flowers. Stems and leaves are edible, steamed or stir-fried.
CINNAMON available both in the piece (called sticks or quills) and ground into powder; one of the world's most common spices.
COCOA POWDER, DUTCH-PROCESSED is treated with an alkali to neutralise its acids. It has a reddish-brown colour, a mild flavour and easily dissolves in liquids.
COCONUT
cream obtained from the first pressing of the coconut flesh alone, without the addition of water; the second pressing (less rich) is sold as coconut milk. Available in cans and cartons from supermarkets.
desiccated concentrated, dried, unsweetened and finely shredded coconut flesh.
flaked dried flaked coconut flesh.

milk not the liquid inside the fruit (coconut water), but the diluted liquid from the second pressing of the white flesh of a mature coconut. Available in cans and cartons at most supermarkets.
shredded thin strips of dried coconut.
CORIANDER [CILANTRO] a bright-green leafy herb with a pungent flavour. Both stems and roots of coriander are also used in cooking; wash well before using. Also available ground or as seeds; these should not be substituted for fresh as the tastes are different.
COUSCOUS a fine, dehydrated, grain-like cereal product made from semolina; it swells to three or four times its original size when liquid is added. It is eaten like rice with a tagine, as a side dish or salad ingredient.
CREAM
pouring also called pure or fresh cream. It has no additives and contains a minimum fat content of 35%.
thick (double) dolloping cream with a minimum fat content of 45%.
CUMIN has a spicy, nutty flavour.
DAIKON this long, white horseradish has a wonderful, sweet flavour. After peeling, eat it shredded and raw in salads, or sliced or cubed and cooked in stir-fries and casseroles. The flesh is white but the skin can be either white or black; buy those that are firm and unwrinkled from Asian food shops.
DIJON MUSTARD pale brown, distinctively flavoured, mild french mustard.
DUKKAH an Egyptian specialty spice mixture made up of roasted nuts, seeds and an array of aromatic spices.
FENNEL a white to very pale green-white firm, crisp, roundish vegetable, about 8–12cm (3¼–4¾in) in diameter. The bulb has a slightly sweet, anise flavour but the leaves have a much stronger taste.
FISH SAUCE called nam pla (Thai) or nuoc nam (Vietnamese); made from pulverised salted fermented fish, most often anchovies. Has a pungent smell and strong taste, so use sparingly.
GARAM MASALA a blend of spices that includes cardamom, cinnamon, coriander, cloves, fennel and cumin. Black pepper and chilli can be added for heat.
GHEE also called clarified butter; with the milk solids removed, this fat has a high smoking point so can be heated to a high temperature without burning.
GOLDEN SYRUP a by-product of refined sugarcane; pure maple syrup or honey can be substituted. Treacle is a similar product; however, it is more viscous and has a stronger flavour and aroma than golden syrup (which has been refined further and contains fewer impurities).
HARISSA a Moroccan paste made from dried chillies, cumin, garlic, oil and caraway seeds. Available from Middle Eastern food shops and supermarkets.
KAFFIR LIME LEAVES also called bai magrood. Aromatic leaves of a citrus tree; two glossy dark green leaves joined end to end, forming a rounded hourglass shape. A strip of fresh lime peel may be substituted for each kaffir lime leaf.
KECAP MANIS a thick soy sauce with added sugar and spices. The sweetness comes from the addition of molasses or palm sugar.
LEMONGRASS a tall, clumping, lemon-smelling and -tasting, sharp-edged grass; the white part of the stem is used, chopped or thinly sliced, in cooking.
LENTILS (red, brown, yellow) dried pulses often identified by and named after their colour. Eaten by cultures all over the world, most famously in the dhals of India, lentils have high food value.
French-style green lentils related to the famous french lentils du puy; these green-blue, tiny lentils have a nutty, earthy flavour and a hardy nature that allows them to be rapidly cooked without disintegrating. Also called australian, bondi or matilda lentils.
LINSEEDS [FLAXSEEDS] slightly larger than sesame seeds and contain high levels of omega-3 fatty acids.
MAPLE SYRUP, PURE distilled from the sap of sugar maple trees found only in Canada and the USA. Maple-flavoured syrup or pancake syrup is not an adequate substitute for the real thing.
MISO fermented soy bean paste. There are many types of miso, each with its own aroma, flavour, colour and texture; it can be kept, airtight, for up to a year in the

fridge. Generally, the darker the miso, the saltier the taste and denser the texture. Salt-reduced miso is available.

MIXED SPICE a classic spice mixture generally containing caraway, allspice, coriander, cumin, nutmeg and ginger, although cinnamon and other spices can be added.

MUSHROOMS

dried porcini also known as cèpes; the richest-flavoured mushrooms. Expensive, but because they're so strongly flavoured, only a small amount is required.

shiitake, fresh also called chinese black, forest or golden oak mushrooms; although cultivated, they are large and meaty, with the earthiness and taste of wild mushrooms.

swiss brown also called cremini or roman mushrooms; are light brown mushrooms with a full-bodied flavour.

NUTMEG a strong and pungent spice ground from the dried nut of an evergreen tree native to Indonesia. Usually found ground, the flavour is more intense from a whole nut, available from spice shops, so it's best to grate your own.

OIL

cooking spray we use a spray made from canola oil unless stated otherwise.

olive made from ripened olives. Extra virgin and virgin are the first and second press, respectively, of the olives; "extra light" or "light" on other types refers to taste not fat levels.

peanut pressed from ground peanuts; most commonly used oil in Asian cooking because of its capacity to handle high heat without burning (high smoke point).

sesame used as a flavouring rather than a cooking oil.

ONIONS

green (scallion) also called, incorrectly, shallot; an immature onion picked before the bulb has formed, has a long, bright-green stalk.

red also known as spanish, red spanish or bermuda onion; a sweet-flavoured, large, purple-red onion.

shallots also called french or golden shallots or eschalots; small and brown-skinned.

PAPRIKA ground, dried, sweet red capsicum (bell pepper); available as sweet, hot, mild and smoked.

PEPITAS [PUMPKIN SEED KERNELS] the pale green kernels of dried pumpkin seeds; available plain or salted.

POLENTA also known as cornmeal; a flour-like cereal made of ground corn (maize). Also the name of the dish made from it.

POMEGRANATE dark-red, leathery-skinned fruit about the size of an orange filled with hundreds of seeds (arils), each wrapped in an edible lucent-crimson pulp with a unique tangy sweet-sour flavour.

PROSCIUTTO a kind of unsmoked Italian ham; salted, air-cured and aged, it is usually eaten uncooked.

QUINOA pronounced keen-wa; is cooked and eaten as a grain, but is in fact a seed. It has a delicate, slightly nutty taste and chewy texture.

RHUBARB long, green-red stalks become sweet and edible when cooked. The leaves are toxic, therefore not edible; trim off and discard the leaves before cutting the stalks.

RICE

arborio small round-grain rice well-suited to absorb a large amount of liquid; the high level of starch make it especially suitable for risottos for its classic creaminess.

basmati a white, fragrant long-grain rice; the grains fluff up when cooked. Wash several times before use.

jasmine is a long-grain white rice recognised around the world as having a perfumed aromatic quality; moist in texture, it clings together after cooking. Sometimes substituted for basmati rice.

ROCKET [ARUGULA] also called rugula and rucola; peppery green leaf eaten raw in salads or used in cooking. Baby rocket leaves are smaller and less peppery.

SEMOLINA coarsely ground flour milled from durum wheat; the flour used in making gnocchi, pasta and couscous.

SESAME SEEDS black and white are the most common of this small oval seed; however, there are also red and brown varieties. The seeds are used as an ingredient and as a condiment.

SOY SAUCE made from fermented soy beans. Several varieties are available in supermarkets and Asian food stores. We use japanese soy sauce unless stated otherwise.

STAR ANISE dried star-shaped pod with an astringent aniseed flavour; used to flavour stocks and marinades. Available whole and ground, it is an essential ingredient in chinese five spice.

STERILISING JARS it's important the jars be as clean as possible; make sure your hands, the preparation area, tea towels and cloths etc. are clean too. The aim is to finish sterilising the jars and lids at the same time the mixture is ready to be bottled; the hot mixture should be bottled into hot, dry, clean jars. Jars that aren't sterilised properly can cause deterioration of the contents during storage. Always start with cleaned washed jars and lids, then follow one of these methods:

(1) Put the jars and lids through the hottest cycle of a dishwasher without using any detergent.

(2) Lie the jars down in a boiler with the lids, cover with cold water, then cover with a lid. Bring to the boil over high heat and boil the jars for 20 minutes.

(3) Stand the jars upright, without touching each other, on a wooden board on the lowest oven shelf. Turn the oven to the lowest possible temperature; leave jars to heat for 30 minutes.

Remove jars from the oven or dishwasher with a tea towel, or from the boiling water with tongs and rubber-gloved hands; the water will evaporate from hot wet jars quite quickly. Stand jars upright, and not touching each other, on a wooden board or a bench covered with a tea towel. Fill jars as directed in the recipe; secure the lids tightly, holding jars firmly with a tea towel or an oven mitt. Leave the jars at room temperature to cool before storing.

SUGAR

brown very soft, finely granulated sugar retaining molasses for its characteristic colour and flavour.

caster (superfine) finely granulated table sugar.

demerara small-grained golden-coloured crystal sugar.

icing (confectioners') also called powdered sugar; pulverised granulated sugar crushed with a little cornflour (cornstarch).

palm also called nam tan pip, jaggery, jawa or gula melaka; made from the sap of the sugar palm tree. Light brown to black in colour and usually sold in rock-hard cakes; use brown sugar instead.

SUNFLOWER SEEDS grey-green, slightly soft, oily kernels; a nutritious snack.

TAHINI a rich, sesame-seed paste.

TOFU also called bean curd; an off-white, custard-like product made from the "milk" of crushed soy beans. Comes fresh as soft or firm, and processed as fried or pressed dried sheets. Fresh tofu can be refrigerated in water (changed daily) for up to 4 days.

TURMERIC is a rhizome related to galangal and ginger. Must be grated or pounded to release its acrid aroma and pungent flavour. Known for the golden colour it imparts, fresh turmeric can be substituted with the more commonly found dried powder. When fresh turmeric is called for in a recipe, the dried powder can be substituted (proportions are 1 teaspoon ground turmeric for every 20g fresh turmeric).

VANILLA

extract obtained from vanilla beans infused in water; a non-alcoholic version of essence.

paste made from vanilla beans and contains real seeds; is highly concentrated: 1 teaspoon replaces a whole vanilla bean. Available in supermarkets.

WATERCRESS one of the cress family, a large group of peppery greens. Highly perishable, so must be used as soon as possible after purchase.

WOMBOK [NAPA CABBAGE] elongated in shape with pale green, crinkly leaves, is the most common cabbage in South-East Asia. Can be shredded or chopped and eaten raw or braised, steamed or stir-fried.

YEAST (dried and fresh) a raising agent used in dough-making. Granular (7g sachets) and fresh compressed (20g blocks) yeast can often be substituted for the other.

YOGHURT, GREEK plain yoghurt strained in muslin to remove the whey, giving it a creamy consistency.

CONVERSION CHART

MEASURES

One Australian metric measuring cup holds approximately 250ml; one Australian metric tablespoon holds 20ml; one Australian metric teaspoon holds 5ml. The difference between one country's measuring cups and another's is within a two- or three-teaspoon variance and will not affect your cooking results. North America, New Zealand and the United Kingdom use a 15ml tablespoon. All cup and spoon measurements are level.

The most accurate way of measuring dry ingredients is to weigh them.

When measuring liquids, use a clear glass or plastic jug with the metric markings.

We use extra-large eggs with an average weight of 60g.

DRY MEASURES

metric	*imperial*
15g	½oz
30g	1oz
60g	2oz
90g	3oz
125g	4oz (¼lb)
155g	5oz
185g	6oz
220g	7oz
250g	8oz (½lb)
280g	9oz
315g	10oz
345g	11oz
375g	(¾lb)
410g	13oz
440g	14oz
470g	15oz
500g	16oz (1lb)
750g	24oz (1½lb)
1kg	32oz (2lb)

LIQUID MEASURES

metric	*imperial*
30ml	1 fluid oz
60ml	2 fluid oz
100ml	3 fluid oz
125ml	4 fluid oz
150ml	5 fluid oz
190ml	6 fluid oz
250ml	8 fluid oz
300ml	10 fluid oz
500ml	16 fluid oz
600ml	20 fluid oz
1000ml (1 litre)	1¾ pints

LENGTH MEASURES

metric	*imperial*
3mm	⅛ in
6mm	¼in
1cm	½in
2cm	¾in
2.5cm	1in
5cm	2in
6cm	2½in
8cm	3in
10cm	4in
13cm	5in
15cm	6in
18cm	7in
20cm	8in
22cm	9in
25cm	10in
28cm	11in
30cm	12in (1ft)

OVEN TEMPERATURES

The oven temperatures in this book are for conventional ovens; if you have a fan-forced oven, decrease the temperature by 10–20 degrees.

	°C (Celsius)	*°F (Fahrenheit)*
Very slow	120	250
Slow	150	300
Moderately slow	160	325
Moderate	180	350
Moderately hot	200	400
Hot	220	425
Very hot	240	475

The imperial measurements used in these recipes are approximate only.
Measurements for cake pans are approximate only. Using same-shaped cake pans of a similar size should not affect the outcome of your baking. We measure the inside top of the cake pans to determine sizes.

INDEX

D

E

F

G

H

I

J

K

L

FIRST PUBLISHED IN 2020 BY ARE MEDIA BOOKS, AUSTRALIA.
THIS EDITION PUBLISHED IN 2022.
ARE MEDIA BOOKS IS A DIVISION OF ARE MEDIA PTY LTD.

ARE MEDIA

Chief Executive Officer Jane Huxley

ARE MEDIA BOOKS

Group Publisher Nicole Byers
Editorial & Food Director Sophia Young
Books Director David Scotto
Creative Director Hannah Blackmore
Managing Editor Stephanie Kistner
Senior Editor Chantal Gibbs
Designer Jeannel Cunanan
Food Editor Cynthia Black

Recipe Developers Rebecca Lyall, Vikki Moursellas, Elizabeth Fiducia, Tessa Immens, Bree Hutchins, Angela Devlin, Charlotte Binns-McDonald, Cynthia Black, Tamika O'Neill

Photographer Alicia Taylor
Stylists Olivia Blackmore, Kate Brown
Photochefs Vikki Moursellas, Elizabeth Fiducia

The publisher would like to thank Thermomix for providing the appliances used for testing the recipes in this book. thermomix.com.au

Printed in China by
1010 Printing International

A catalogue record for this book is available from the National Library of Australia.
ISBN 9781925866612 (paperback)

Published by Are Media Books, a division of Are Media Pty Ltd, 54 Park St, Sydney; GPO Box 4088, Sydney, NSW 2001, Australia
Ph +61 2 9282 8000
www.awwcookbooks.com.au

International rights enquiries
internationalrights@aremedia.com.au

Order books
Phone 1300 322 007 (within Australia) or order online at www.awwcookbooks.com.au
Send recipe enquiries to recipeenquiries@aremedia.com.au